engage

C000277389

Put your guard up — this issue of **engage** is hard-hitting. We'll see Jesus offending people; God punishing rebellious kings; Paul straight-talking; and we'll discover how to fight for the faith. Also, we'll meet the Dark Destroyer who found the light and we'll learn all about our spiritual enemies.

✴ **DAILY READINGS** Each day's page throws you into the Bible, to get you handling, questioning and exploring God's message to you — encouraging you to act on it and talk to God more in prayer.

THIS ISSUE: Meet Jesus, the King of controversy in **Matthew;** watch as Israel and Judah destroy themselves in **2 Kings;** learn life lessons from Paul in **2 Corinthians;** and fight for the faith with **Jude.**

✴ **TAKE IT FURTHER** If you're hungry for more at the end of an **engage** page, turn to the **Take it further** section to dig deeper.

✴ **REAL LIVES** True stories, revealing God at work in people's lives. This time — **we meet the brutal boxer who found Jesus.**

✴ **TRICKY** tackles those mind-bendingly tricky questions that confuse us all, as well as questions our friends bombard us with. This time we ask: **Can we really trust the Bible?**

✴ **ESSENTIAL** Articles on the basics we really need to know about God, the Bible and Christianity. This issue, we look at what the Bible says about **spiritual enemies.**

✴ **STUFF** Articles on stuff relevant to the lives of young Christians. This issue: **we give advice on talking to non-Christian relatives.**

✴ **TOOLBOX** is full of tools to help you understand the Bible. This issue we look at different **Bible translations.**

All of us who work on **engage** are passionate to see the Bible at work in people's lives. Do you want God's word to have an impact on your life? Then open your Bible, and start on the first **engage** study right now...

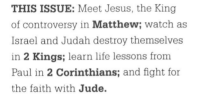

HOW TO USE engage

1 Set a time you can read the Bible every day

2 Find a place where you can be quiet and think

3 Grab your Bible, pen and a notebook

4 Ask God to help you understand what you read

5 Read the day's verses with **engage**, taking time to think about it

6 Pray about what you've read

BIBLE STUFF

We use the NIV Bible version, so you might find it's the best one to use with **engage**. If the notes say **"Read Matthew 15 v 1–9"**, look up Matthew in the contents page at the front of your Bible. It'll tell you which page Matthew starts on. Find chapter 15 of Matthew, and then verse 1 of chapter 15 (the verse numbers are the tiny ones). Then start reading. Simple.

In this issue...

FIGHTING IN THE ENGAGE CORNER...

Wrangling writers: Martin Cole   Cassie Martin   Carl Laferton   Helen Thorne
Dastardly designer: Steve Devane
Power-punching proof-readers: Anne Woodcock   Nicole Carter
Exhausted editor: Martin Cole (martin@thegoodbook.co.uk)

Matthew

King of controversy

Many people picture Jesus as a laidback, gentle hippy. Always preaching love and tolerance. Always being nice. Never being controversial or offensive. But that's not the Jesus Matthew tells us about.

As we immerse ourselves in Matthew's story, we'll meet a Jesus who regularly clashes with religious authorities, offends "holy" people and points out hypocrisy. We'll meet a Jesus who goes against what society expects — he meets with and accepts those who "respectable" people shunned and avoided.

We'll meet a Jesus who fought demons. We'll meet a Jesus who said unpopular and controversial things about religion, divorce, heaven and hell.

We'll meet a Jesus who didn't come to be warm and fuzzy all the time. We'll meet a Jesus who said shocking things and made people feel uncomfortable; who people hated because His words were hard to swallow. We'll meet a Jesus who came to die.

As Matthew takes us into the intimate life story of Christ, we won't meet a wishy-washy do-gooder. We'll meet the all-powerful, Satan-slaying Son of God. This is someone we must take very seriously. Because, if you let Him, Jesus will change your life.

1 | Blind faith

The Pharisees thought they were the true leaders of God's people. They thought they were God's favourites. But Jesus was about to show them up for who they really were. The controversy kicks off immediately.

👁 Read Matthew 15 v 1–9

ENGAGE YOUR BRAIN

▶ What accusation was made? (v2)

▶ How did Jesus respond? (v3)

▶ How were these men being hypocritical? (v4–6)

▶ What was true about their religion and teaching? (v8–9)

Jesus pointed out how the Pharisees made up ridiculous rules that actually stopped people from serving God and honouring their parents! He showed up their "religion" for the sham it was — they were all talk and their hearts were not devoted to God (v8).

👁 Read verses 10–20

▶ What were the disciples worried about? (v12)

▶ How did Jesus describe the Pharisees? (v14)

▶ What did Jesus say makes people unclean? (v18–20)

The Pharisees were focusing on man-made rules. But they weren't concerned about their hearts, their thoughts or their words — the important stuff. These supposedly holy leaders were like the blind trying to lead the blind, and the result would be spiritual disaster.

THINK IT OVER

▶ In what ways do you concentrate on keeping rules or appearing good rather than dealing with your evil thoughts?

▶ What specific stuff do you need God's help to deal with?

PRAY ABOUT IT

Talk to God about these things. Thank Jesus for coming into the world to deal with the problem of our hearts.

➡ TAKE IT FURTHER

Grab some more on page 107.

2 | Gone to the dogs

More controversy today. A woman comes up to Jesus, begging him to heal her demon-possessed daughter. What do you think Jesus' response will be?

👁 Read Matthew 15 v 21–28

ENGAGE YOUR BRAIN

- ▶ *Where was this woman from? (v22)*
- ▶ *What was surprising about Jesus' response? (v23)*
- ▶ *And the disciples' response? (v23)*
- ▶ *Why wouldn't Jesus heal her daughter? (v24)*
- ▶ *What do you think v26 means?*
- ▶ *And what was the women's brilliant answer? (v27)*
- ▶ *What was the happy ending to this controversial story? (v28)*

Jesus was now in a Gentile (non-Jewish) area. The Jews were God's chosen people. So when this Gentile woman asked Jesus for help, His answer was simple — I came for the Jews, not Gentiles. It wouldn't be fair to put other people ("dogs") before God's chosen ones. But the woman seemed to know Jesus' mission was far wider reaching than to just the tiny Jewish nation.

The message of Jesus is for everyone. All types of people from every kind of background can get to know God through Jesus. His death made it possible for anyone to be part of God's chosen people.

GET ON WITH IT

- ▶ *If Jesus' message is for everyone, what does that mean for you?*
- ▶ *And what does that mean for the people you see regularly?*
- ▶ *If Jesus' message is for everyone, what does that mean Christians should do?*
- ▶ *What will YOU do, exactly?*

PRAY ABOUT IT

Thank God for the people who told you about Jesus. Now talk to God about your answers to the above four questions.

THE BOTTOM LINE

The message of Jesus is for everyone.

➔ TAKE IT FURTHER

The great commission — page 107.

3 ¦ Sign language

Today's story sounds very familiar. Jesus had recently fed over 5000 Jewish people with a few loaves and fish. This time, He does the same thing for Gentiles.

👁 Read Matthew 15 v 29–39

ENGAGE YOUR BRAIN

▷ *What did Jesus do on the mountainside? (v30)*

▷ *How did these Gentiles react? (v31)*

▷ *What did this show about Jesus? (v32)*

These non-Jews saw Jesus' miracles and were amazed. They even praised the God of Israel! Unheard of! As we saw yesterday, Jesus' message is for everyone. He has compassion (v32) for everyone.

👁 Read Matthew 16 v 1–4

▷ *What did the Jewish leaders demand? (v1)*

▷ *How did Jesus ridicule their request? (v2–3)*

▷ *How did He describe them? (v4)*

▷ *What sign would He give them?*

The Pharisees were the ultra-religious group who made up loads of extra rules to live by. The Sadducees were another Jewish group, who said there was no life after death. The Pharisees and Sadducees were enemies — opposed to each other's teaching — yet they were united in hating Jesus.

Jesus had done so many incredible things already — seeing one more miracle would not have caused these stubborn men to accept Jesus. They were out to get Him. But Jesus saw through their demands. The only sign they would see would be Jesus dying and rising again 3 days later. If you're not sure why that's called the sign of Jonah, go to *Take it further*.

PRAY ABOUT IT

These men were seen as holy and religious yet they rejected Jesus. Instead, Jesus would save many outsiders. Thank God that Jesus came for outsiders like us. Pray that you won't assume you're good enough for God.

→ TAKE IT FURTHER

Follow the signs to page 107.

4 ┆ Stale bread ┆

The disciples had seen Jesus feed thousands of people with just a tiny amount of bread (and fish). Twice. And they'd seen the Pharisees and Sadducees fail to believe Jesus. But the disciples still missed the point...

👁 Read Matthew 16 v 5–7

ENGAGE YOUR BRAIN

▷ *What mistake had the disciples made? (v5)*

▷ *What did Jesus warn them? (v6)*

▷ *But what were they more worried about? (v7)*

It's like a sitcom joke. These 12 guys had just witnessed two incredible food miracles, with basketfuls of bread left over. And what do they do? Leave their packed lunch at home! So Jesus takes this opportunity to warn them about false teaching. But the disciples miss the point. Again.

👁 Read verses 8–12

▷ *Why didn't they need to worry about having no food? (v8–10)*

▷ *What should they be more concerned about? (v11–12)*

Yeast is used in baking bread, to help dough rise. You add a little bit of yeast and it spreads through the whole batch of dough. In the same way, wrong teaching, from religious leaders who refused to recognise Jesus' identity, was getting everywhere. See how Jesus sadly had to describe the disciples (v8).

THINK IT OVER

▷ *In what areas of life do you need to trust Jesus more?*

▷ *Do you believe everything you're taught about Christianity and spirituality?*

▷ *How can you check that what you're being taught is true?*

PRAY ABOUT IT

Ask God to help you trust in Him to provide for your needs. And pray that you won't fall for false teaching that leads you away from God.

→ TAKE IT FURTHER

Spot false teachers on page 107.

5 | Jesus jigsaw

Since the beginning of his book, Matthew has been building up a picture of who Jesus is. Like a jigsaw — slotting the different parts of the picture together. But the disciples couldn't put the picture together. Until now.

👁 Read Matthew 16 v 13–17

ENGAGE YOUR BRAIN

▶ What was the public opinion about Jesus ("the Son of Man")? (v13–14)
▶ What did Peter realise? (v16)
▶ What did Jesus think of this answer? (v17)

Peter realised that Jesus was both God and human in one person. God's chosen Messiah was in town: the Rescuer and Ruler who God had promised would come. This is the one the Old Testament had pointed to; the one everyone was waiting for!

👁 Read verses 18–20

▶ What did Jesus say about Peter and about the church? (v18)
▶ What surprising thing did Jesus say to His disciples? (v20)

Verse 18 means Jesus will build His church on the apostles' (Peter and co) true teaching about Jesus. And the church will never be destroyed by the devil! (For more on confusing v19, go to *Take it further*.)

Peter finally realised who Jesus is but Jesus told His disciples not to tell anyone. The Jews expected the Christ to be a mighty warrior who'd free them from the Romans. Imagine what would have happened if word got out that the Christ was here! But Jesus wasn't that kind of Messiah. The disciples had to learn why Jesus had come before they could start talking about Him. That comes tomorrow.

PRAY ABOUT IT

Tell Jesus your own reply to v15. Don't just repeat the "right" words, tell Him everything. Ask Him to help you understand.

THE BOTTOM LINE

Jesus is the Christ, the Son of the living God.

→ TAKE IT FURTHER

Verse 19 explained on page 108.

6 | Cross words

Peter must have been feeling great — he'd finally realised that Jesus is God's Son, the Christ. And Jesus gave Peter a great job. But there was loads Peter still hadn't grasped about Jesus. Vital stuff.

👁 Read Matthew 16 v 21–23

ENGAGE YOUR BRAIN

▶ What had Jesus come to do? (v21)

▶ What do you think of Peter's reaction?

▶ What did Jesus think of it? (v23)

Earlier, the devil had tried to tempt Jesus to abandon His mission. This mission required Jesus to die for sinners like us. It's understandable that Peter didn't want his friend and master to suffer and die. But Peter wasn't seeing the big picture. Jesus came to die on the cross. It was essential and would be glorious.

👁 Read verses 24–28

▶ What does Jesus expect of His disciples? (v24–25)

▶ Why is it vital to make the right decision about believing and following Jesus? (v27)

Back then, if you saw someone carrying a cross, you knew they were heading towards their death. "Denying yourself" means exactly that: giving up the right to live. Being prepared to live for Jesus, whatever the cost. Even if that means suffering or death.

There's no other way to follow Jesus. He went to the cross and He expects us to give everything for Him. It's the route to life, true life.

PRAY ABOUT IT

Maybe it's time to ask God's forgiveness, and to help you realise who Jesus really is. And to get back to making Jesus everything you live for. Talk to God about it right now.

THE BOTTOM LINE

If anyone would come after me, he must deny himself and take up his cross and follow me.

→ TAKE IT FURTHER

A little bit more on page 108.

7 ┊ Mountain tension

Chapter 16 was a rollercoaster for the disciples. A real high point was realising who Jesus is. A downer when they learned what He'd come to do. The the twist of what it would mean to follow Him. Now for more thrills and spills.

👁 Read Matthew 17 v 1–8

ENGAGE YOUR BRAIN

▷ *What amazing thing did Peter, James and John witness? (v2)*

▷ *Who else was present? (v3)*

▷ *What did God the Father say about Jesus? (v5)*

▷ *And what must Jesus' followers do? (v5)*

Jesus was "transfigured": His whole appearance changed (v2). Ever looked directly at the sun? That's how Jesus was — dazzlingly pure, glorious, unique. And then they heard God's voice, confirming that Jesus really was His Son. So they should listen to Him. And so should we.

👁 Read verses 9–13

▷ *What did Jewish law experts claim? (v10)*

▷ *What was Jesus' answer to this? (v11–13)*

The Jews believed (from Malachi 4 v 5) that Elijah would return before the arrival of God Himself. Jesus says that John the Baptist was the "Elijah" who prepared the way for Jesus. Most of the people didn't realise his importance, just as they rejected Jesus and would kill Him (v12).

GET ON WITH IT

▷ *How can you make sure you don't make the same mistake and ignore Jesus?*

▷ *How will you make sure you listen to His words?*

▷ *Which of His commands do you need to take more seriously?*

PRAY ABOUT IT

Talk to God about your answers.

→ TAKE IT FURTHER

More mountain tension on page 108.

8 ⌐ Demon disarray ¬

Peter, James and John are walking down the mountain with Jesus, having just seen something amazing. But they're soon brought back to earth with a thump.

👁 **Read Matthew 17 v 14–18**

ENGAGE YOUR BRAIN

▶ *What was the double problem?*
v15:
v16:

▶ *What was Jesus' reaction to His disciples' inability to heal the boy?*

▶ *Was it a problem for Jesus? (v18)*

Watch out when life is going well. A high spiritual experience is often followed by a crashing low. Here, Jesus came down the mountain to see His disciples in a mess.

👁 **Read verses 19–21**

▶ *Why couldn't they drive out the demon?*

▶ *What can real faith in God achieve?*

The disciples should have trusted Jesus' power and authority. Even a little faith can move obstacles that seem immovable. God can do great things through us if we trust Him to.

👁 **Read verses 22–23**

▶ *What did Jesus tell His disciples again?*

▶ *How did they react?*

It's incredibly sad that Jesus was betrayed and had to suffer and die. But we don't need to be grief-filled like the disciples. We know that Jesus died to rescue us and He was raised back to life (v22) and rules in heaven!

PRAY ABOUT IT

Say sorry to God for times you've shown no faith in Him. Ask Him to increase your faith and trust in Him so you can serve Him better. And thank Him for Jesus' death and resurrection.

THE BOTTOM LINE

Real faith can move mountains.

➔ **TAKE IT FURTHER**

Faith the facts on page 108.

9 | Fishy funds

Ever heard people complain about paying taxes? Maybe you pay them yourself and you notice the huge chunk they take out of your wages. At least that's something Jesus, God's Son, doesn't need to bother with. Well, actually...

👁 **Read Matthew 17 v 24–26**

ENGAGE YOUR BRAIN

▶ What did the tax collectors quiz Peter about? (v24)

▶ What's the answer to Jesus' strange question? (v25–26)

▶ Any idea what point Jesus was making?

Of course kings don't collect taxes from their own sons. That would be crazy. Jewish people had to pay temple tax. The money was used to look after God's temple. Jesus was God's Son, so it was ridiculous to ask Him to pay taxes for His Father's temple. But most people didn't believe Jesus was God's Son.

👁 **Read verse 27**

▶ How did Jesus get the money to pay the tax?

▶ Why did Jesus pay the tax?

The money that Jesus paid would go to the temple and to the Jewish leaders who would eventually torture and kill Him. Jesus was contributing towards His own death. But He knew He had to die as part of His Father's perfect plans. And He paid the taxes so as not to offend anyone. Sometimes we have to give up our rights if it helps God's work.

THINK IT OVER

▶ Do you sulk or put up a fight when it comes to paying money you owe?
▶ Or what about doing chores?
▶ How does your attitude affect how others view your faith?

PRAY ABOUT IT

Ask God to help you make wise decisions and not cause unnecessary trouble or offence. And thank Him for Jesus' great wisdom and power.

➔ **TAKE IT FURTHER**

No *Take it further* section today.

10 Who's the greatest?

Jesus talked last time about tax, where big guys in authority grab money from little people. Maybe that's what nudged the disciples to ask about authority — who are the big guys in God's kingdom?

Read Matthew 18 v 1–4

ENGAGE YOUR BRAIN

▶ *What surprising thing did Jesus do when they asked this big question? (v1–2)*

▶ *What's shocking about Jesus' words? (v3)*

▶ *So who's the greatest? (v4)*

Children were unimportant in that society: to be looked after, but not to be looked up to. Jesus' action (v2) was shocking, His teaching (v3–5) even more so. Disciples should be like children — insignificant, unimpressive, willing to be nobodies.

Such a change isn't just for those who already follow Jesus. It's the only way to become a Christian — realising you're nothing without Jesus.

Read verses 5–6

▶ *So what should we do for humble Christians? (v5)*

▶ *But what's the big warning? (v6)*

Christians shouldn't put themselves first. They must be welcoming towards other believers, not leading other Christians astray.

GET ON WITH IT

Write down specific ways you can...

a) show more humility

b) be more welcoming and inclusive

c) stop doing stuff that causes others to sin

PRAY ABOUT IT

Only you know what you need to talk to God about today.

THE BOTTOM LINE

Be childlike — humble, welcoming, and innocent.

→ TAKE IT FURTHER

Great expectations on page 109.

11 | Cut it out

More controversial teaching from Jesus. He's not used many picture stories recently. But today we've got arm chopping, eye gouging and sheep chasing!

👁 **Read Matthew 18 v 7–9**

ENGAGE YOUR BRAIN

▶ If something in your life causes you to sin, what should you do with it?

▶ Why?

Hacking legs off and throwing them in the river sounds drastic! But Jesus isn't saying we should actually chop off body bits! He's saying we must try to *cut out* the things in our life that cause us to sin.

GET ON WITH IT

▶ What do you read / watch / listen to that you shouldn't?

▶ Which friendships lead you towards sin?

▶ What exactly will you do to cut sin out of your life?

👁 **Read verses 10–14**

▶ What should be our attitude towards younger/weaker Christians? (v10)

▶ Why? (v14)

Sometimes we're also tempted to look down on and gossip about Christians who are wandering away from God. But God never gives up on them (v14), so neither should we. Pray for such people and think of ways to bring them back.

PRAY ABOUT IT

Ask God to help you cut out from your life those things that cause you to sin. Then spend time praying for younger Christians you know, that they'll grow as believers. And for friends who are wandering away from God's way.

→ **TAKE IT FURTHER**

The final cut — page 109.

12 | Clashing Christians

Would you forgive a Christian friend if they... a) wore embarrassing clothes in your company? b) borrowed and broke your phone? c) upset your closest friend? d) humiliated you publicly? e) apologised for any of these?

How big is your forgiveness? Jesus talked last time about care for "little ones" — ordinary Christians. Now He says what to do when they mess up and commit sin.

👁 **Read Matthew 18 v 15–18**

ENGAGE YOUR BRAIN

▶ *If another Christian wrongs you, what should you do first? (v15)*

▶ *And if that fails? (v16)*

▶ *And if that fails? (v17)*

Don't rush up to others to retaliate. Our main concern shouldn't be for revenge or getting what's best for ourselves. We should want to help other Christians when they sin, so they keep living God's way. If you talk over your differences and the other person continues sinning, only then should you bring in other people. We must pray about the situation too...

👁 **Read verses 19–20**

▶ *What's the great promise here?*

▶ *How does v20 transform small Christian meetings?*

Presumably, the two or three were meeting to pray for the wrongdoer. But the principle goes wider — where a handful of Christians gather in Jesus' name, agree and pray, then He is with them. And God will answer!

We can sometimes get down if our youth group or school Christian meeting only has a few people in it. But even in tiny groups, Jesus is there with His followers!

PRAY ABOUT IT

Pray for any Christian friends you've fallen out with. Ask God to help you deal with the situation in a godly way. And pray for Christian groups and meetings you attend. That you'd remember Jesus is with you.

→ **TAKE IT FURTHER**

More on page 109.

15

13 : Don't forget to forgive

How forgiving are you? If someone wrongs you or upsets you, how willing are you to forgive them? And what if someone repeatedly lets you down?

Read Matthew 18 v 21–22

ENGAGE YOUR BRAIN

> How many times should we forgive someone?

Jesus doesn't mean literally that number of times. It's hard to forgive people who've upset us or treated us really badly. Especially if it happens again and again. But Jesus says we should forgive them over and over, without end. And here's why.

Read verses 23–35

> How big was the debt the king cancelled?
> What punishment should he have received? (v25)
> What did the man do with his own debtor? (v28–30)
> What should he have done and why? (v32–33)
> So what happened to him? (v34)
> What's the message to us? (v35)

It seems crazy. This guy is let off a staggeringly huge debt that would have led to him losing his family. But when someone owes him a small amount, he goes bananas.

This is a picture of Christians. God has forgiven them for their terrible sins. They deserved death and hell but, because of Jesus, He forgives them completely. When people wrong us or upset us, it's nowhere near as bad as how we've treated God. So we should forgive them, just as God forgives us. Over and over again.

GET ON WITH IT

> Who do you need to show forgiveness to?
> Which broken relationship do you need to mend right now?

PRAY ABOUT IT

Thank God for His incredible forgiveness. Ask Him to help you show His attitude of forgiveness when people mess you around.

→ TAKE IT FURTHER

Don't forget to turn to page 109.

14 | The D-word

"There are two sides to every argument and they're usually married to each other." Sadly, for many, marriage is no laughing matter. Many marriages are in trouble or end in divorce. It can tear families apart.

👁 Read Matthew 19 v 1–6

ENGAGE YOUR BRAIN

▷ What did the Pharisees want to know? (v3)

▷ How did Jesus answer them?

The Pharisees were hoping Jesus would disagree with Old Testament teaching and get Himself in trouble. Jesus simply pointed out God's plan for marriage — a husband and wife are joined together and shouldn't be separated.

👁 Read verses 7–9

▷ What was their next question, and Jesus' answer? (v7–8)

▷ What controversial thing did Jesus say about divorce? (v9)

The Pharisees claimed that Moses commanded divorce. Jesus replied: "Not at all. He'd only reluctantly permitted it." Like it or not, God's principle is that marriage is for life.

Anyone who gets divorced thinking there's an escape clause is wrong. Jesus only allows divorce if your partner commits adultery.

👁 Read verses 10–12

▷ What conclusion did the disciples come to? (v10)

▷ Did Jesus agree?

Jesus says marriage isn't for everyone — so we shouldn't obsess about finding a husband/wife. Some people will serve God better if they stay single. Others will serve Him in their marriages.

PRAY ABOUT IT

Pray for people who are suffering because of family break-up (maybe that's you). Ask God to be at the centre of their lives. And pray for married couples you know — that they will never want to give up.

→ TAKE IT FURTHER

Kid's stuff is on page 109.

15 | Money talks

"What must I do to get eternal life?" "If I keep the Ten Commandments, will that get me into heaven?" How would you answer these questions? Let's check out Jesus' answers.

👁 Read Matthew 19 v 16–22

ENGAGE YOUR BRAIN

▶ *What's wrong with the man's question? (v16)*

▶ *How did Jesus answer him? (v17–19)*

▶ *What did the guy claim? (v20)*

▶ *How did Jesus pull the rug out from under his feet? (v21)*

▶ *What was this man's main problem? (v22)*

This young man rates himself highly — he rolls up thinking what good deed he can do to gain eternal life. Jesus' reply (v17): "You want to know about good and bad? Try God's standards then — to be good enough for Him means keeping the 10 Commandments. Can you do that?"

Jesus then gives him commandments 5–9 and a summary: "Love your neighbour as yourself."

▶ *Could he have kept all these?*

▶ *Could you?*

None of us is good enough to earn eternal life. We've all sinned and sin stops us being good enough. Only Jesus can help us, if we turn to Him for forgiveness.

This man actually seems to believe he's kept God's commands. But Jesus knows better: "You want to be perfect? Then cut your love of money by giving it away and set your heart on following me." Money, relationships, job, sport, studies — none of these should get in the way of your love for Jesus.

PRAY ABOUT IT
Talk to God honestly about anything He's put on your heart today.

➔ TAKE IT FURTHER
More money stuff on page 109.

18

16 ¦ Mission possible ¦

Yesterday we met a young guy who seemed to have it all — he was rich and lived a good life. But he wouldn't put Jesus first. Sad. Jesus now has more to say on wealth and what He expects from His followers.

👁 Read Matthew 19 v 23–26

ENGAGE YOUR BRAIN

▶ What controversial thing did Jesus say? (v23–24)

▶ How did the disciples react? (v25)

▶ And what other incredible truth did Jesus speak? (v26)

The common view was that if you were rich, it must be because God liked you. But money can take over people's lives and become more important to them than God. That doesn't mean rich people *can't* become Christians. **Nothing** is impossible for God. We can't earn our way into heaven (with money or living a good life). Only Jesus can rescue us.

👁 Read verses 27–30

▶ What does Jesus expect from His followers? (v27, 29)

▶ What will be their reward? (v29)

▶ When will they receive it? (v28)

Being a Christian is costly. Sometimes we'll lose friends because we love Jesus. We also have to turn away from the things that used to be more important to us than Jesus. But one day, when Jesus returns, we'll be rewarded far more than we could ever imagine! The Christian life isn't easy, but it's definitely worth it.

THINK IT OVER

▶ Do you care too much about money and possessions?

▶ What can you do to make sure God is more important to you than other stuff?

▶ In what situations will it help to remember that nothing is impossible for God?

→ TAKE IT FURTHER

A little bit more on page 110.

REAL LIVES

Dark Destroyer finds the light

Nigel Benn was a devastating boxer. His professional career began with a streak of 22 consecutive knockout wins, earning him the terrifying nickname of the Dark Destroyer. Benn went on to become world champion at both middleweight and super middleweight, boxing in some of the most memorable contests of the era.

EMPTY SUCCESS

He made millions, drove fast cars, lived in big houses, and achieved hero status in the boxing ring, yet Nigel describes his achievements as nothing in comparison to life today. In a dramatic turnaround, one of Britain's best ever boxers has swapped training for prayer, and fighting for preaching. Benn says: "The Dark Destroyer is long gone; he's now here to destroy the darkness and that's it!"

"People say to me, 'Nigel, you've achieved so much in life, you were two times world champion!' But I match that up with the Bible and what Jesus says in Mark 8 v 36: *'What good is it for a man to gain the whole world, yet forfeit his soul?'* I've done all that — I forfeited my soul, my mind, my will and my emotions.

What did it profit me? Absolutely nothing! Now I can read the word of God and match myself up with it. Jesus has shown me how to help people, people who are stuck in that dark pit but who really need help.

"Being world champion means nothing; they're just pieces of metal. People say I've achieved so much but for me to achieve something would be to help a drug addict get free, help someone with marriage problems or to help someone who is just struggling with life. That's what Jesus has called me to do."

ROCK BOTTOM

Nigel revealed that where many sportsmen looked to drink and drugs in pursuit of happiness, his constant battle was sex. Hooked on casual sex, his addiction made him so depressed he tried to commit suicide. In a bout of self-pity, he took an overdose and tied a hosepipe to his car's exhaust in an attempt to end his life. But, in what Nigel describes as a miracle from God, the hose fell out of the car three times and his life was spared.

Nigel, who knocked out 35 opponents in 42 professional fights, immediately realised it was God who had saved his life. Following countless affairs which led to well-publicised bust-ups and rows with his wife, he realised he had to confess all to the woman he loved. "I wasn't a happy man. I was hurting my wife by having affairs and was out partying. There was something missing in my life. I was going down that road of destruction and didn't know how to get out of it.

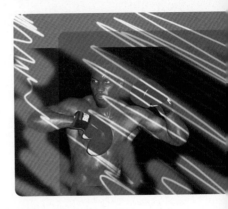

NEW START

"When the hose came out of the car three times, I had an encounter with Jesus. He was showing me that He was there for me. However, people can shout 'Hallelujah' and praise God but still be walking in darkness. That was me for some years.

"I had to go and tell my wife I was having an affair, which was hard. I could have lost everything — my wife, my kids — but it was like: 'Satan, you don't have a hold on me no more'. Jesus had set me free!

FROM DARKNESS TO LIGHT

"If you read the Bible it says: *'God is light; in him there is no darkness.'* And: *'If we claim to be without sin, we deceive ourselves and the truth is not in us. If we confess our sins, he is faithful and just and will forgive us'.* (1 John 1 v 5, 8–9)

"I want to tell people what Jesus Christ has done in my life. I want to show people that Jesus is the way, He is the truth and He is the life. Without Him I would not be here today.

"A lot of people have this stereotype about Christians where they think Christianity is so boring, but I want to show them the light. We will have problems and temptations but God will always make a way for us to get out of it. If I'm able to help save one soul, then that is what God has called me to do. I don't care if I offend people; I would rather offend people than my Father in Heaven."

Interview from www.newlife.co.uk

2 Kings

Decline and fall

In issue 14 of *engage*, we were astounded by the drama of 1 Kings. After King Solomon, God's people had split into two kingdoms — Israel (in the north, its capital Samaria) and Judah (in the south, its capital Jerusalem). The action in 1 & 2 Kings switches between these two kingdoms.

2 Kings is 1 Kings part 2 — it's all one story, the sorry history of God's Old Testament people under the rule of kings. 2 Kings covers the period from about 850 to 580BC, history buffs.

God's Old Testament people were unique in history, because God chose to share His presence with that nation. God lived among them — His temple in Jerusalem was proof of that. But its kings were (mostly) leaders who couldn't care less about God. Their big error, repeated over and over, was to ignore God's covenant: His promise to give His people a great life when they obey His laws.

God sent prophets (like Elijah and Elisha) to warn His people not to neglect the covenant agreement. But the warnings were ignored and these kings sent God's people into a sinful slide that would bring them crashing down.

As you read this royal blockbuster:
• observe God in the driving seat of history
• notice how powerful His words are
• watch God not afraid to judge His people
• see God keeping promises He made centuries earlier
• listen to God calling His people to love Him back
• and see how the shocking history of God's people under bad human kings points to the need for a perfect King from God.

17 | Flaming fireballs!

2 Kings begins in Israel with a king called Ahaziah (see the last few verses of 1 Kings). And with a prophet called Elijah. If we wanted to sum up this whole book, then chapter 1 is 2 Kings in a nutshell.

👁 Read 2 Kings 1 v 1–8

ENGAGE YOUR BRAIN
▶ What had happened to King Ahaziah? (v2)
▶ What did he foolishly do? (v2)
▶ What should Elijah's question have made the king realise? (v3)
▶ What would happen to Ahaziah? (v6)

God won't tolerate "pick and mix" religion, where people sometimes obey Him but also worship other gods and superstitions.

👁 Read verses 9–18
▶ What did the king do next? (v9, 11, 13)
▶ What was Elijah's response? (v10, 12)
▶ What did the third captain get right? (v13–14)
▶ What did Elijah do? (v15–16)
▶ And what happened? (v17)

See how wrong the king's attitude was? He thought he'd challenge God and argue with God's decision. Idiot. Only God's mercy prevented more fireball fury. Nothing else is worth knowing about Ahaziah. He's to be remembered only for failing to obey God.

And that's the nutshell. In 2 Kings, we'll meet more kings who (apart from a few) think they can choose from any number of gods. We'll see God speaking through His prophets, calling His people back to living His way. And we'll watch kings brushing off God's warnings and bringing God's judgment on themselves.

PRAY ABOUT IT
Think what parts of God's character this chapter reminds us of. Praise God that He is just and fair, and thank Him for being patient with His people.

→ TAKE IT FURTHER
Firefighting fun on page 110.

23

18 | Chariot of fire

Have you ever seen a plane take off and disappear into the sky? What about a human? No? Well, get ready to see Elijah fly to heaven with a chariot of fire.

👁 **Read 2 Kings 2 v 1–10**

ENGAGE YOUR BRAIN

▶ *What did young Elisha repeatedly say to his master? (v2, 4, 6)*

▶ *What did all the local prophets know? (v3, 5)*

▶ *What did Elisha want? (v9)*

Elijah couldn't promise this to Elisha as it was for God to give such a thing to His people.

👁 **Read verses 11–18**

▶ *What did Elisha see? (v11–12)*

▶ *What sign did God give Elisha that his request of v9 had been granted? (v14–15)*

▶ *What hadn't the others understood? (v16–18)*

The future looked bleak without God's messenger, Elijah, around any more. But we should rely on God, not on particular "holy" people. The Lord would now use young Elisha as His messenger and would do great things through him.

It's easy to idolise Christian leaders. But we should remember it's God who does great things. He often uses His people to do them, but it's God who has the power. God is in control.

THINK IT OVER

▶ *How have you seen God's power at work? (It could be through small things and answers to prayer, not just spectacular stuff.)*

PRAY ABOUT IT

Thank God that He's so mighty, powerful and in control. Pray for Christian leaders you know, that God would use them to do His work.

➔ **TAKE IT FURTHER**

No *Take it further* today.

19 Dirty water and bear attacks

God's prophet, Elijah, has been taken up to heaven in a fiery chariot. Now his servant, Elisha, will take on the role of God's messenger. Today's two tales show us that God was on his side.

👁 **Read 2 Kings 2 v 19–22**

ENGAGE YOUR BRAIN

▶ *What was the problem? (v19)*

▶ *What did Elisha use to fix it?*

▶ *Who was behind it all? (v21)*

The area around Jericho was nice, but the water supply was lethal, killing both humans and animals. God had cursed the area because the people of Jericho had once been hugely sinful. But now God turns His curse into a blessing. Here, God's word through God's prophet brings God's grace to God's people.

👁 **Read verses 23–25**

▶ *What are your instant thoughts on this strange story?*

Bethel was well known for idol worship. God's prophets were not popular there. A large group of young lads came out of the town to taunt Elisha. They insulted him and told him to get lost. They were hassling God's messenger and that's a very foolish thing to do. Elisha cursed these lads and two bears mauled 42 of them.

This sounds harsh but God had warned people what would happen if they turned against Him: *"'If you remain hostile toward me and refuse to listen to me ... I will send wild animals against you, and they will rob you of your children."* (Leviticus 26 v 21–22)

God brings healing to those who accept Him, but punishment to those who reject Him.

PRAY ABOUT IT

Thank God that He saves everyone who trusts Him. Thank Him that He rightly punishes sin. Pray for people you know who continue to mock and reject God, that they would turn to Him and accept His healing.

➔ **TAKE IT FURTHER**

Bear necessities are on page 110.

20 Three kings

Time for another wild story involving Elisha and the kings of Judah and Israel. This one includes a blood-effect sunrise, floods in a desert, child sacrifice and an angry sheep breeder.

👁 Read 2 Kings 3 v 1–12

ENGAGE YOUR BRAIN

▶ How is Israel's King Joram described? (v2–3)

▶ What was Joram's problem? (v4–6)

▶ Who did Joram ask for help? (v7, 9)

▶ How was Jehoshaphat different from Joram? (v11–12)

👁 Read verses 13–27

▶ What were Elisha's different attitudes to Joram and Jehosh'?

▶ What two promises did God make? (v17–18)

▶ How did they come true? (v20–25)

Elisha saw Joram for the fake he was. He worshipped false gods, not the one true God. Yet the Lord did amazing things for these three kings because one of them (Jehoshaphat) served Him. God made astonishing promises and then He kept them. In fact, God used the flooded desert to win the war (v22–24). Yet the success wasn't total.

God always keeps His promises — both to bless His people and to punish His enemies. And He often gives far more than He's promised.

PRAY ABOUT IT
Think back to times you've prayed and God has done far more than you expected. God hears our prayers and often answers them in surprising and generous ways. Remember this as you bring your thanks and requests to Him right now.

→ TAKE IT FURTHER
More on baffling v26–27 on p110.

21 | More 'mazing miracles

What an action-packed life! Elisha has already healed poisoned water, set bears on an angry mob, insulted a king and watched his boss fly up to heaven. And God has loads more gobsmacking things in store for Elisha.

👁 **Read 2 Kings 4 v 1–7**

ENGAGE YOUR BRAIN
▶ *What was the tragic situation?*
▶ *How did Elisha solve it?*

As always, God is overflowing with kindness for His people.

👁 **Read verses 8–17**
▶ *What great thing did the wealthy woman do for Elisha? (v8–10)*
▶ *What great thing did Elisha ask God to do for her? (v16)*
▶ *How did she react and what happened? (v16–17)*

As always, God is overflowing with kindness for His people.

👁 **Read verses 18–37**
▶ *What happened to this miracle boy? (v20)*
▶ *What did his mother say to Elisha? (v28)*
▶ *What did Elisha do? And what was the result? (v29–31)*
▶ *What did Elisha do next? (v32–33)*

▶ *What happened? (v34–37)*

God gave a wonderful gift to this woman and then took it away from her. No wonder she was distressed (v28) — her hopes had been raised only to be dashed. Yet she still clung on to God's prophet to do something about it. After Gehazi's failed attempt, Elisha went to the dead boy and cried to God for help. And God brought the lad back to life.

Sometimes we don't understand why God does certain things. But we must cling on to our trust in Him. The God who raised the boy back to life also raised Jesus back to life. And one day all Christians will be raised to eternal life with Him.

PRAY ABOUT IT
Thank God for His incredible love and kindness — shown perfectly in Jesus' death and resurrection for us.

⤳ **TAKE IT FURTHER**
Follow the leader to page 111.

22 | Fantastic food phenomena

What's the most memorable meal you've had? Maybe it was a special occasion. Or just the tastiest thing you've ever eaten. Or maybe something surprising happened. Elisha was about to have two very eventful meals.

👁 Read 2 Kings 4 v 38–41

▷ What was the situation in the Gilgal area? (v38)

▷ Yet what did Elisha ask for?

▷ What was the problem? (v39–40)

▷ What did Elisha do?

Bible experts think this poisonous plant was a small yellow melon that's a laxative and can be fatal. Nasty. Elisha used a very simple thing — flour — to combat the poison. God can use the simplest of things to do His amazing work.

👁 Read verses 42–44

▷ What present did Elisha receive?

▷ What "impossible" thing did he want to do with it? (v42–43)

▷ Why? (v43)

▷ What happened? (v44)

There were 100 hungry men but only 20 small loaves. But just a few words from God were enough to turn them into a filling meal with leftovers! God's word can do things that seem impossible. If it's a choice between what you can see with your eyes and what God promises, take God's word.

This story also points us to Jesus miraculously feeding thousands with just a few fish and loaves. God can do things we think are impossible. Especially through Jesus — He can even save sinful fools like us and use us in His plans!

PRAY ABOUT IT

▷ Is there anything you think is impossible to pray for?
Thank God that His word is always true and trustable. And talk to Him about things you think seem impossible — maybe certain friends or family becoming Christians.

➔ TAKE IT FURTHER

Feed your face on page 111.

23 | A clean start

Crusty scabs, flaky skin, itchy swellings and white spots. All over your body. That's leprosy, and it's seriously unpleasant. Today, we'll scratch beneath the surface of four characters — Elisha, Naaman, Gehazi and God.

👁 **Read 2 Kings 5 v 1–7**

ENGAGE YOUR BRAIN

▷ *What are we told about Naaman? (v1)*

▷ *What did the Israelite slave girl suggest? (v3)*

▷ *How did the King of Israel (Joram) react? (v7)*

▷ *How much did he trust God?*

👁 **Read verses 8–14**

▷ *What did Elisha do? (v8–10)*

▷ *What made Naaman angry? (v11–12)*

▷ *But what happened? (v13–14)*

👁 **Read verses 15–27**

▷ *What did Naaman realise? (v15)*

▷ *What did Elisha say to Naaman's offer of gifts? (v16)*

▷ *But what did Gehazi do?*
v20:

v22:

v25:

▷ *What was the result? (v27)*

Gehazi's punishment was fair. Ever since the time of Abraham, God had promised to be Israel's God — to lead them and live among them. Such a privilege brought responsibility: obeying God would bring His blessing; disobeying Him would bring His judgment. So Gehazi's punishment wasn't harsh; it was God acting in line with His covenant.

One of God's people was punished. Yet a diseased outsider received God's healing. This story reminds us that *anyone* can turn to God to be healed of their sin sickness. And it reminds us that God's people (Christians) must keep living God's way.

➔ **TAKE IT FURTHER**
Soily stuff on page 111.

Axe of kindness

Ever feel alone or that the Christian life is just too hard? Today, Elisha reminds us that Christians have God on their side, even when they don't see it. Believers are never alone.

👁 Read 2 Kings 6 v 1–7

ENGAGE YOUR BRAIN

▷ *What was the first problem and the solution? (v1–2)*

▷ *What was the second problem and the solution? (v5–7)*

This may seem like a tiny thing to worry about. But this guy had lost something he'd borrowed and couldn't afford to pay back the owner. He was worried and needed help. He told Elisha, and God rescued the axe-head. God cares about our worries and even about the "small" things in our lives. He's on our side.

👁 Read verses 8–23

▷ *What did Elisha keep doing? (v10)*

▷ *So what did the King of Aram do? (v13–14)*

▷ *Why didn't Elisha's servant need to be afraid? (v15–17)*

▷ *What did God do for Elisha and for Israel? (v18, 23)*

God was doing amazing things for Elisha and for Israel. He told Elisha all about the King of Aram's secret attack plans so Elisha could warn King Joram of Israel. And then God protected Elisha in a miraculous way — surrounding him with an angelic army and blinding his enemies.

It's easy to feel alone as a Christian, but we're not alone. God is on our side, helping us and protecting us. We may not always see or realise this, but it's OK to ask God to show us.

PRAY ABOUT IT

Thank God that He's on the side of all Christians and cares about their lives. Tell Him about any worries or genuine needs you have. And if you feel alone, ask God to show you that you're not.

→ TAKE IT FURTHER

A little bit more on page 112.

25 Famine and fortune

King Ben-Hadad of Aram is determined to crush the Israelites. God keeps protecting Israel, but their king, Joram, refuses to turn to God or to trust His prophet, Elisha. Even during a horrendous siege and famine.

👁 **Read 2 Kings 6 v 24 – 7 v 2**

ENGAGE YOUR BRAIN

▷ What effect did the siege have on Samaria? (v25–28)
▷ How did King Joram respond? (v30–31)
▷ What did God tell Elisha?
v32:
v1–2:

It's a hideous picture. Ben-Hadad trapped the people in Samaria for so long that they ran out of food. Donkey's heads and "seed pods" (probably dove dung!) were being sold as food for ridiculous amounts of money. People were killing and eating their children. Disgusting. The Israelites were desperate, yet the king still didn't turn to God for help. But God would rescue them anyway.

👁 **Read 2 Kings 7 v 3–20**

▷ How did God keep His promise?
v6–7:
v16:
v17–20:

▷ Did King Joram believe it? (v12)

Yet again, God uses outsiders such as lepers in His impressive plans. God had terrified the Arameans (v6–7) and then these lowly lepers delivered the good news. Time and time again, God uses the weak in His plans.

God kept His promise to rescue the people, and also to punish the unbelieving officer (v19–20). God always keeps His word — to rescue His people and punish those who refuse to believe.

THINK IT OVER

▷ Ever think God couldn't use you?
▷ Ever look down on other people as useless?
▷ Ever doubt God's word?

PRAY ABOUT IT

▷ Talk these things over with God.

🔎 TAKE IT FURTHER

No Take it further today.

26 ¦ More bad kings

Remember the wealthy woman who built a room in her house for Elisha? God gave her a son who then died but was brought back to life. Well, she's about to re-enter the story.

👁 Read 2 Kings 8 v 1–6

ENGAGE YOUR BRAIN

▶ How had Elisha shown kindness to this family? (v1–2)

▶ How was God's timing perfect? (v3–6)

👁 Read verses 7–15

▶ What did the king of Aram surprisingly do? (v7–8)

▶ What would happen? (v10)

▶ What upset Elisha? (v11–12)

▶ What happened? (v15)

Years earlier, God gave Elijah the job of anointing three kings who would punish God's people for their disobedience (1 Kings 19 v 15–17). One of those kings was Hazael, and here Elijah's servant, Elisha, is carrying out God's instructions. It tore Elisha apart because he knew Hazael would do hideous things to God's people.

But they'd refused to turn back to God and so would be punished.

👁 Read verses 16–29

▶ What was Jehoram like as a king? (v18)

▶ But what's the incredible truth about God in v19?

▶ Was Ahaziah any better? (v27)

The kings of Judah turned away from God. Yet God remembered His covenant with David and didn't destroy despicable Judah (v19). God would protect David's line of kings. Centuries later, David's greatest descendant, Jesus, would be the greatest King ever.

PRAY ABOUT IT

Thank God that, despite our sin and disobedience, He still loves us and sent Jesus to be the perfect King.

→ TAKE IT FURTHER

Grab some more on page 112.

27 | Hired hitman

The next tale in this book of Kings is the story of Jehu. As usual, it's full of surprises and weird stuff — a shock announcement, betrayal, archery, regicide (king killing), and blood-spattering violence. Not for the faint-hearted.

👁 Read 2 Kings 9 v 1–13

ENGAGE YOUR BRAIN
▶ What did God do through Elisha? (v1–3)

▶ What would God do through Jehu? (v6–10)

Just as God told Elijah, he'd wipe out Ahab's family for their refusal to live under God's rule. It was judgment deserved. Next, it's judgment delivered... first against Israel's King Joram and Judah's King Ahaziah.

👁 Read verses 14–29
▶ Why was God doing all this? (v22)

▶ How was God keeping His promise to King Ahab? (v24–26)

👁 Read verses 30–37
▶ Why did Jezebel meet such a gruesome end? (v36–37)

Sometimes it seems that evil people get away with their crimes. But God will punish them in the end. King Ahab and Queen Jezebel had committed some horrible crimes, yet were still wealthy and successful. But, in the end, they met the same fate as anyone who goes against God and His people. They were punished. God won't tolerate sin — people living their own way instead of His.

THINK IT OVER
▶ What have you learned about God and His justice today?

▶ How should this affect your view of life?

TALK IT OVER
If anything from today's passage (or 2 Kings generally) bothers or baffles you, grab an older Christian and ask them to open the Bible with you and explain it to you.

➔ TAKE IT FURTHER
More on Jezebel's demise on p112.

28 | Heads will roll

Jehu was called by God to be Israel's king and to carry out God's fierce judgment. But by the end of chapter 10, we'll see it's not all yahoo for Jehu. Warning: viewers may find the following scenes disturbing.

👁 **Read 2 Kings 10 v 1–17**

ENGAGE YOUR BRAIN

▷ *How did Jehu get Israelite leaders to do his dirty work? (v1–7)*

▷ *What did Jehu say had happened? (v10)*

▷ *What else did he do? (v13-14, 17)*

It's grisly stuff, but God had said it would happen. Ahab had repeatedly sinned against God, often in disgusting ways. God promised that Ahab's family would be destroyed. And that's what Jehu did.

👁 **Read verses 18–36**

▷ *How did Jehu deceive the servants of false god Baal? (v18–25)*

▷ *What happened to Baal's temple and to Baal worship? (v27–28)*

▷ *What did God say to Jehu? (v30)*

▷ *How did Jehu mess up? (v29, 31)*

▷ *What did this lead to? (v32)*

God continued to punish Israel, here using Jehu to dish out His judgment. But Jehu made no attempt to stop Israel two-timing God (v29). How long would God let this continue?

THINK IT OVER

▷ *How do you two-time God?*
▷ *What stops you from serving Him wholeheartedly?*
▷ *How does God feel about sharing top spot with other things?*
▷ *What do you need to do?*

PRAY ABOUT IT

It's time for a heart-to-heart with God. Pour it all out to Him.

THE BOTTOM LINE

God demands to be number one.

➔ **TAKE IT FURTHER**

Roll over to page 112.

29 ¦ Kid for king ¦

While Jehu was sword-waving and slaughtering in Israel, over in Judah, Ahab and Jezebel's daughter, Athaliah was running wild. She totally lost it when Jehu killed her son, Judah's King Ahaziah. More slaughter is on the menu.

👁 Read 2 Kings 11 v 1–21

Athaliah wanted to rule Judah and so tried to destroy the rest of the royal family, so she'd have no competition. Even though God had appointed that royal family. Thankfully, it wasn't a total massacre, as Jehosheba rescued baby Joash.

👁 Read verses 4–16

▶ *What controversial thing did Jehoida organise? (v12)*

▶ *What two things did he give young Joash? (v12)*

▶ *How did Athaliah react? (v13–14)*

▶ *What happened to her? (v16)*

👁 Read verses 17–21

▶ *What important thing did the people do? (v17)*

▶ *What else? (v18)*

▶ *How was Judah transformed? (v20)*

Brilliant. Evil Athaliah was ousted, 7-year-old Joash was made king and the people of Judah committed themselves to living God's way. They also destroyed everything related to worshipping idols. Turning back to God means fully committing yourself to Him and kicking out anything that gets in the way.

GET ON WITH IT

▶ *Do you need to re-commit yourself to God?*

▶ *What can you do to live more for Him?*

▶ *What "idols" do you need to throw out of your life?*

Talk to God about these things.

THE BOTTOM LINE

Committing to God means smashing the idols in your life.

→ TAKE IT FURTHER

More about this on page 113.

Can we trust the Bible?

The conversation normally goes something like this...

You don't trust the Bible, do you?
Depends what you mean by trust! It can't tell me how to bake a cake (it's not a recipe book). It can't help me pass my science exam (because it's not a textbook). But here's what the Bible claims it can do:

- *"The Holy Scriptures [ie: the Bible] are able to make you wise for salvation through faith in Christ Jesus"* (2 Timothy 3 v 15) — it tells us how we can live for ever.

- It's *"useful for teaching, rebuking, correcting and training in righteousness"* (v16) — it tells us how we can best live today.

How do you know you can trust what it says about those things?

Because it's written by God! In between those two sentences telling us what the Bible is for, we

read something mindblowing: *"All Scripture is God-breathed"* (v16). The Bible's like a manual on life, the universe and everything, written by the Maker of life, the universe and everything. If anyone knows how to live for ever, and how to live today, it'll be the Creator God! The Bible's trustworthy, because God wrote it.

Ah, but did God write it?
Let me give you three reasons why we know God wrote the Bible, each really important:

1. HISTORICAL

The Bible is a work of history. One of the human writers of the Bible said the things he wrote about have been *"handed down to us by those who from the first were eye-witnesses ... I myself have carefully investigated everything"* (Luke 1 v 2–3). Other historical works and archaeological discoveries support the claim that the Bible is talking about real history. You can investigate that, as many other people have.

If we live as if the Bible is God's words to us, we find that the Bible works. It makes sense of life, of what the world is like, and of who we are. It explains why we ask questions about God and death and beyond: God has *"set eternity in the hearts of men"* (Ecclesiastes 3 v 11). Why not ask some big questions and listen seriously to the Bible's answers?

3. GOD SAYS SO

Imagine you get a letter from your aunt. How would you know it's from her? Because it says so! There may be other clues — it was posted near where she lives, it has details about your aunt's life. But ultimately, you trust it's from your aunt because she tells you it's from her — in the letter.

And while history and experience suggest the Bible is God's word, ultimately the only clincher is what God says. He's the only One who knows whether or not He wrote the Bible! And He says it is His word — in His word, the Bible.

Hmmm... I'm still not convinced.

Think about this — if the Bible really is written by God, then we can trust everything in it. If the Bible's trustworthy, it's great news — it means that knowing Jesus is all you need to have purpose in life today, and perfect life for ever. That's what the Bible tells us.

But it's also challenging news — because it says you do need Jesus. It says you don't rule your life and future — Jesus does. That means that instinctively, at this moment, you'd rather the Bible wasn't written by God, so you can carry on ruling your own life. Be careful you don't let your feelings get in the way of the facts!

Have you actually read the Bible? Lots of people dismiss it without looking at it. Don't knock it till you've tried it. Let me give you one of the books that are in the Bible — a Gospel, a historical biography of Jesus.

If you do have this kind of conversation with someone, and they agree to read a Gospel, why not read it with them? A booklet which will help you do that is: one2one Just Looking — grab a copy at www.thegoodbook.co.uk or www.thegoodbook.com

2 Corinthians

Power in weakness

Have you ever turned on a movie halfway through? Or tuned into a soap you haven't watched for a while? Confusing, isn't it? "Who is that again? I thought she was with that guy — why is she kissing his brother? Didn't he leave to become a dentist?" Sometimes your favourite character seems to have turned into an entirely different actor!

Well, 2 Corinthians is a bit like that — we're coming in halfway through this church's relationship with the apostle Paul, and unless we know the back story, it can get very confusing! Let's fill in the gaps:

Paul told people in Corinth the gospel and they became Christians — yay! (Acts 18 v 1–18)

Paul wrote to them to encourage them (we don't have this letter but it's mentioned in 1 Corinthians 5 v 9). They wrote back. Nice. (Referred to in 1 Corinthians 7 v 1).

Paul sent them another letter, which we know as 1 Corinthians. But by this point lots is going wrong in the Corinthian church — mixed-up ideas and all sorts of dodgy behaviour (why not read 1 Corinthians, if you haven't already?).

His letter did not go down well and things were still a mess, so Paul visited in person to try and sort things out (see 2 Corinthians 2 v 1). Things were still pretty dire so he sent them a bit of a howler (see 2 Corinthians 2 v 3–4, 2 v 9 and 7 v 8).

Paul wondered whether he should visit again, but instead wrote them a letter, 2 Corinthians (finally!) He also deals with some new problems in this letter, as we'll find out...

He also visited them again (Acts 20 v 2–3) after he wrote this letter.

Phew! Clear as mud? Let's read on!

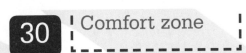

30 Comfort zone

Paul's relationship with the Corinthian church wasn't exactly perfect. But he loved them deeply and he wanted them to love Christ deeply. Despite their doubts about him and personal attacks, he still cared enough to write.

👁 Read 2 Corinthians 1 v 1–2

ENGAGE YOUR BRAIN

▶ Who gives Paul his authority?
▶ Who does the Corinthian church belong to?

The new problems in the Corinthian church were partly due to newcomers questioning and attacking Paul and what he taught. Here, Paul is gently reminding the Corinthians of who he is and who sent him.

👁 Read verses 3–5

▶ Which words occur most often in verse 3–7?
▶ What is Paul thankful for? (v3–4)
▶ What is the key to understanding suffering? (v5)

PRAY ABOUT IT

Have you really taken on board the fact that following Jesus will involve suffering? Pray that God would help you to understand that and be prepared for it while not being overwhelmed — knowing that

Jesus will comfort you and help you through it.

👁 Read verses 6–11

▶ What benefit does Paul see in his sufferings? (v6–7)
▶ Have times of suffering ever helped you like this?
▶ How tough was Paul's situation in v8–9?
▶ What good came out of that situation? (v9–11)

PRAY ABOUT IT

Do you know anyone who is suffering at the moment? If not, someone you know, then how about Christians in other countries who are persecuted? Pray for them that they would fully rely on "God, who raises the dead".

THE BOTTOM LINE

The pattern of the Christian life is suffering then glory.

→ TAKE IT FURTHER

Comforting words on page 113.

31 Yes man

The Corinthians had badly misjudged Paul. Here he takes the opportunity to set the record straight AND put the focus back on Christ.

👁 Read 2 Corinthians 1 v 12–17

ENGAGE YOUR BRAIN

▶ Why does Paul have a clear conscience? (v12–14)

▶ What might the Corinthians have been thinking about him?
v13:
v17:

Paul wasn't being indecisive or unreliable by changing his travel plans. Nor was he trying to confuse them in his letters.

👁 Read verses 18–20

▶ How has God kept His promises?

THINK AND PRAY

Let verse 20 sink in for a moment. All of God's promises are "yes" in Christ. Think about what that means — can you list some promises from the Old Testament? Jesus fulfils them all — He is the ultimate "yes man". Thank God right now.

👁 Read verses 21–22

▶ What does Paul remind the Corinthians about God?

▶ What do the Corinthians and Paul have in common?

GET ON WITH IT

How will verses 21–22 help you to stand firm as a Christian when you're at home/school/college/work with non-Christian friends and family?

THE BOTTOM LINE

All God's promises are "yes" in Christ.

TAKE IT FURTHER

Say "yes" for more — page 113.

32 | Forgiveness

Paul's last visit to the Corinthians hadn't been much fun. Someone in the church had done something pretty awful and as a result, Paul had to show some tough love. They were probably still feeling a bit sore....

👁 Read 1 v 23 – 2 v 11

▷ What reason does Paul give for not having come to Corinth as he'd originally planned? (v23)

▷ What reaction should the church provoke in Paul? (1 v 24 – 2 v 3)

▷ What reaction have they actually caused by their behaviour? (v1-4)

▷ How would you sum up Paul's attitude to the Corinthian church in v1–11?

▷ What is the impact of serious sin on the whole church? (v5)

▷ How should the church respond? (v6–8)

▷ Why? (clue in v10)

▷ Why else? (v11)

GET ON WITH IT

Forgiving people isn't easy. Especially when they have hurt us or done something really bad. But like Paul — we need to forgive in the sight of Christ. Why? Think of all that Jesus has forgiven us for when He died on the cross.

▷ Who do you need to show forgiveness to?

PRAY ABOUT IT

Satan likes nothing better than a divided church full of bitter people who won't forgive (v11). Pray for unity in your church. Pray that people would forgive each other in Jesus' name and be united around His gospel — the message of Jesus.

THE BOTTOM LINE

Forgive us our sins as we forgive those who sin against us.

→ TAKE IT FURTHER

A little more is on page 113.

33 | Smell of success

What's your favourite smell? And what smells make you want to vomit? Paul says that Christians are "the aroma of Christ" to people. The way we live affects how others view Jesus.

👁 Read 2 Corinthians 2 v 12–13

ENGAGE YOUR BRAIN

▶ *Why did Paul go to Troas? (v12)*
▶ *Why couldn't he relax?*

Titus was delivering Paul's strongly worded letter to the Corinthians and Paul was anxious to find out how they'd received it. Despite his anxiety, Paul was still sharing the good news about Jesus.

👁 Read verses 14–17

▶ *Who is behind this task of spreading the gospel? (v14)*
▶ *Where is the gospel heard (or smelled!)? (v14–15)*

PRAY ABOUT IT

The way Christians live is like a nice smell for some people. But for others who reject Jesus we're a rotten stink! Even so, pray that you'll keep spreading the aroma of Christ.

▶ *Who enables Paul and his fellow apostles to do the task? (v17)*

▶ *What is the reaction from those who hear? (v16)*

TALK IT OVER

Chat to another Christian about people you know and their reactions to Jesus. It seems weird that some people respond to the gospel with such joy while others are so hostile. But we shouldn't be surprised (v16).

👁 Read 3 v 1–6

Recent newcomers to the church brought letters from others to try to prove how successful and important they were. The transformation of the Corinthians into believing Christians was sufficient evidence of God's work in them through Paul's teaching. Only God can change hearts and lives.

THE BOTTOM LINE

You are the fragrance of Christ.

TAKE IT FURTHER

Smell you later! Page 113.

34 | Glory story

Compare and contrast! In one corner we have the old covenant, or law, given through Moses, and in the other corner we have the new covenant — all about Christ and sealed by the Holy Spirit.

👁 **Read Exodus 34 v 29–35**

👁 **Then 2 Corinthians 3 v 7–18**

God gave His people the Ten Commandments and made a covenant agreement with them at Mount Sinai, way back in the book of Exodus. The problem was that the Israelites couldn't keep God's rules. They couldn't live His way and the covenant simply stood as a reminder of their failures — it condemned them. These new teachers in Corinth were trying to get the Corinthian Christians to go back to Moses and the old covenant.

ENGAGE YOUR BRAIN

▷ How glorious was the old covenant? (v7)

▷ What about the new covenant? (v8–9)

▷ How much better is following Christ than following the law? (v10–11)

▷ What is the drawback of only following the old covenant? (v14–15)

▷ What are the benefits of the new covenant? (v16–18)

The old covenant was merely a shadow of the reality in Christ. Going back to the law is like watching a trailer rather than the film itself.

PRAY ABOUT IT

Thank God that in following Christ you are not only made righteous, but you can see God's plan clearly, and by His Spirit you are becoming gloriously more and more like Jesus, whose glory never fades.

THE BOTTOM LINE

We reflect God's glory.

TAKE IT FURTHER

More O.T. stuff on page 114.

43

35 | See the light

It must have been tempting for Paul to have felt downhearted and discouraged as his critics attacked him and his ministry. But he didn't lose heart. Here's why:

👁 Read 2 Corinthians 4 v 1–2

ENGAGE YOUR BRAIN

▶ *Sum up his approach to sharing the gospel in verse 2:*

Paul is not trying to trick or manipulate people when he shares the gospel with them. He knows that God has given him this task and God is watching him, so he'll do it honestly and clearly.

GET ON WITH IT

Are you ever tempted to soften certain parts of the gospel message? Leave out things you know people won't like? Or promise more than the Bible does? Read verse 2 again and let that shape your behaviour.

👁 Read verses 3–6

▶ *Who blinds people to the truth of God's rescue plan? (v4)*

▶ *Who do you think Paul is talking about?*

▶ *Who makes people "see" spiritually? (v6)*

▶ *Who is the gospel all about and what is He like? (v4–6)*

God brought light into the world at the creation. In sending Jesus, it's like a second creation: God awakening us to see Jesus as He really is — Lord of all. The devil (v4) blinds unbelievers; God makes them see (v6). Brilliant!

PRAY ABOUT IT

Pray for your friends and family who don't know Jesus, that God would shine His light in their hearts so they see the glory of God — Jesus Christ.

THE BOTTOM LINE

Jesus is God's glory. See the light.

→ TAKE IT FURTHER

Follow the light to page 114.

36 | Jars of clay

Just in case they still haven't got the message, Paul reminds the Corinthians that the gospel is not about him or any other impressive leader, but about Jesus Christ. Well, obviously.

👁 Read 2 Corinthians 4 v 7–12

ENGAGE YOUR BRAIN

▶ *Looking back at the previous few verses, what is this treasure that Paul is talking about in v7?*

▶ *What do you think the "jars of clay" refer to?*

As Christians, we have a priceless treasure to proclaim in the gospel. But we are very weak. Paul acknowledges this but says it doesn't matter — in fact, it simply shows even more how wonderful God is!

▶ *How does Paul feel about his situation? (v8–9)*

▶ *What has he learned about what Jesus is doing in him? (v10–11)*

▶ *What is the result for others? (v12)*

Paul's reliance on God kept him going in tough situations. Sharing in Jesus' sufferings (v10) also meant that Paul experienced Jesus' resurrection power. When we are at our limit, humanly speaking, it is only God who gets the glory for keeping us going.

PRAY ABOUT IT

Ask God to be glorified in your weakness. Be specific — maybe you find it hard to keep going as a Christian. Maybe you feel far too shy to share the gospel with your friends or you don't know what to say. His all-surpassing power is there for you!

THE BOTTOM LINE

We are weak, but God's power is immense.

→ TAKE IT FURTHER

More power in weakness on p114.

37 | What really matters?

What really matters to you? What makes you get up in the morning? What is your favourite topic of conversation? What are you prepared to suffer for?

👁 Read 2 Corinthians 4 v 13–15

ENGAGE YOUR BRAIN

▶ *Why does Paul speak out about the gospel? (v13)*

▶ *What is it that he believes? (v14)*

▶ *Do you believe that?*

One day, just like Jesus, we will be raised from the dead and will meet our Maker. That fact shaped everything Paul did and spoke about. For some it will be a day of great joy, and for others it will be a terrible day.

👁 Read verses 16–18

▶ *How does Paul cope with suffering now? (v16–17)*

▶ *What really matters to Paul? (v18)*

Ask yourself those questions again:

▶ *What makes you get up in the morning? Your mum? Or setting your alarm to read the Bible?*

▶ *What is your favourite topic of conversation? TV last night or Jesus Christ?*

▶ *What are you prepared to suffer for? Expensive beauty treatments, sports training sessions or being mocked for going to church?*

▶ *Is it obvious that you follow Christ or do you look just like all your non-Christian friends?*

PRAY ABOUT IT

Pray now for friends and family who don't know Jesus as their King. Pray that, like Paul, you would be shaped by what you believe and that you would speak out about it. Ask God to help you fix your eyes on the unseen, eternal future rather than the temporary now.

THE BOTTOM LINE

I believe, therefore I speak.

→ TAKE IT FURTHER

Grab some more on page 114.

38 | Paul gets in tents

How do you feel about camping? Maybe you're a really healthy type who can't get enough of the great outdoors. Or perhaps the thought of sleeping in a chilly tent with rain dripping through a hole makes you feel ill.

👁 Read 2 Corinthians 5 v 1–5

ENGAGE YOUR BRAIN

▷ What do you think Paul is talking about when he talks about these different buildings in v1–5?

Our bodies that are weak (see chapter 4 v 7) and mortal will one day be replaced by new, resurrection bodies like Christ's, that will be imperishable and will never die.

▷ What is so great about the future body waiting for Christians? (v1)

▷ How does Paul know for sure there is a better body waiting for him after death? (v5)

PRAY ABOUT IT

As Christians, we can be confident that we have a glorious resurrection body waiting for us after death or when Jesus returns. But facing our current bodies aging and dying is still not much fun. Pray for any elderly Christians you know — that they

would trust in this glorious promise of a new, perfect body.

👁 Read verses 6–10

▷ What does Paul want? (v6–8)

▷ What is Paul's priority whether alive now or in the future? (v9)

▷ What future event does Paul again focus on that shapes his life now? (v10)

GET ON WITH IT

▷ How will you focus more on your perfect future than on your imperfect present?

▷ How exactly will you try to please God more this week?

THE BOTTOM LINE

We live by faith, not sight.

→ TAKE IT FURTHER

Carry on camping on page 115.

39 | The gospel truth

Have you ever thought of yourself as an ambassador? That's how Paul sees his job – but being God's ambassador is less about dinner parties and drinks receptions, and more like peace negotiations and reconciliation.

Read 2 Corinthians 5 v 11–15

ENGAGE YOUR BRAIN

▶ What motivates Paul and what does he do as a result? (v11)

▶ What does Paul want the Corinthians to understand about him? (v12–14)

▶ What effect should Christ's death have on Christians? (v15)

The word "compels" in verse 14 is very strong. Imagine you're holding a bar of soap and your hands are wet. What happens when you squeeze your hands together? The bar of soap shoots up into the air. That is how strongly Christ's love compels Paul. Understanding the gospel means he can't do anything but tell others about it (v15).

PRAY ABOUT IT

Someone once said the reason we don't tell our friends about Jesus is because either we don't believe the gospel or we don't love our friends enough. Think that through and talk to God about it.

Read 5 v 16 – 6 v 2

▶ What is so amazing about what the gospel achieves? (v17)

▶ What is the gospel? (v18–19, 21)

▶ How is God spreading the gospel? (v18–20)

▶ When does God want people to respond? (6 v 1–2)

▶ Have you done that?

Reconciliation is God restoring the friendship with Him that we broke by sinning. Jesus became like us (treated by God as His enemy) so that we might become more like God!

PRAY ABOUT IT

Thank God for reconciling you to Himself by Jesus taking your sins so you could have His righteousness. You are a new creation!

→ TAKE IT FURTHER

Find more truth on page 115.

40 ┊ PSALMS: Praise God!

Time for some psalms. This one has David bursting with praise for God's love and compassion. A few definitions: **iniquities, transgressions = disobeying God; covenant, precepts = God's laws; dominion = rule, authority.**

👁 Read Psalm 103

Read all of Psalm 103 in one go. Grab some spare paper and write down everything you can find about a) what God is like; b) what God does.

Next, read it in chunks. After each one, write down one truth about God you want to remember.

v1–2:

v3–7:

v8–14:

v15–18:

v19–22:

ENGAGE YOUR BRAIN

▶ *What's David's attitude to God?*

▶ *Are you ever like this? Why / why not?*

▶ *Which verses show God's great generosity?*

▶ *Which show His great power?*

▶ *What does David say God has done in the past?*

▶ *How does this give you confidence for the future?*

▶ *Using this psalm, summarise what God's like in five words:*

THINK IT OVER

▶ *Which verses talk of how God's people should live?*

▶ *Is this how you're living?*

PRAY ABOUT

Now use parts of Psalm 103 as you praise and thank God for who He is and what He's like.

→ TAKE IT FURTHER

Raise the praise on page 115.

49

41 Creation celebration

Even been amazed at the world or the universe?
Did you say: a) "Wow, what an amazing world!" and leave it at that?; b) "Aren't humans great for discovering this?"; c) How amazing God is for making all this!

👁 Read Psalm 104 v 1–18

ENGAGE YOUR BRAIN

▶ What are some of the amazing things God has done?
v5:

v6–8:

v10–12:

v14–15:

👁 Read verses 19–30

▶ What else has God done?
v19–22:

v24–25:

▶ What is God's relationship with all He has created? (v27–30)

God didn't just create the world and then leave it alone. These verses show God is intimately involved in the daily life and sustaining of all creatures. Our lives depend completely on God — eating, breathing, everything.

👁 Read verses 31–35

▶ What's the purpose of God's creation? (v31)

▶ How should we respond to our awesome God? (v33–34)

▶ What was David's attitude to those who didn't worship God? (v35)

Someone once said: "The whole purpose of humans is to glorify God and to enjoy Him for ever". Fantastic, isn't it? People are made in God's image and can know God personally. But they're also to blame for turning away from Him (v35).

PRAY ABOUT IT

Next time you're out and about, marvel at the world God's made. Think what this says about God's character. And do the right thing and praise Him for it.

➔ TAKE IT FURTHER

Get creative on page 115.

42 | Faithful Father

It's time for a history lesson. This psalm sings about specific things God did for His Old Testament people, the Israelites. And it points to how God deals with and cares for His people today.

👁 **Read Psalm 105 v 1–7**

ENGAGE YOUR BRAIN

▶ How should we respond to all that God had done for us?
v1:
v2:
v3:
v4:
v5:

👁 **Read verses 8–22**

▶ From Israel's history, what is the psalmist especially thankful for?
v8–11:
v12–15:
v17–22:

👁 **Read verses 23–45**

▶ What else?
v23–38:
v39–41:
v42–45:

▶ How should God's people respond to all He's done? (v45)

Link v42–44 with v11. God kept His holy promise (v42). This psalm is underlining God's total faithfulness down the centuries. He does what He says. He sticks by His people. And He always will. The only right way to respond is to show our love for Him by submitting to His rule. Obeying Him. Living God's way.

THINK IT OVER

▶ How do you need to respond to God after reading this psalm?

▶ How should it affect the way you live?

PRAY ABOUT IT
Read verses 1–5 again and do what they say.

➔ **TAKE IT FURTHER**
More on page 116.

Resident evil

In *Essential*, we take time out to explore key truths about God, the Bible and Christianity. This issue we look at the controversial topic of spiritual enemies. What's the Bible say?

They're the stuff of cartoons, horror movies and electronic games: Satan, demons and all things evil. We get used to seeing them as computer-generated images. But are they real? And if they are, how should we think about them?

The Bible teaches us that much of the spiritual world is beautiful. There are loads of angels busy praising God (Isaiah 6 v 1–3) and helping Christians serve Jesus better (Hebrews 1 v 14). But some of the spiritual world is ugly. Satan and his demons are actively trying to mess up God's plans. These evil beings are:

REAL

Satan and his demons truly exist. Jesus was sure of that. At the beginning of time God created the physical world (which we can see) and the spiritual world (which we can't) and everything was wonderful (Genesis 1 v 3). But some angels became proud and rebelled against God (Jude 6) — they became demons.

ACTIVE

These demons don't deny that God exists. They know He is all powerful (James 2 v 19). But they try to stop His work anyway. It was Satan, in the form of a serpent, who tempted the first woman, Eve, to disobey God (Genesis 3 v 1–7). It was Satan who tried to persuade Jesus that He didn't need to go through with His plan of salvation (Luke 4 v 1–13). And it is Satan and his followers who try to stop people today from living God's way. They do that by making it hard for non-Christians to understand how great God is (2 Corinthians 4 v 4; Mark 4 v 15) and encouraging Christians to believe things that aren't true (1 Timothy 4 v 1).

DEFEATED

The activity of the evil ones can seem a bit scary but the good news is that their power is totally rubbish when compared to God's! Satan has only ever had limited authority (Job 1 v 12) and since Jesus came to earth, the devil's influence has been cut even more.

Satan didn't manage to persuade Jesus to give up on His plan to save people (Luke 4 v 12). Throughout His ministry, Jesus showed He had authority over evil (Mark 1 v 21–27; 5 v 1–20; 9 v 14–32). And when Jesus died on the cross and rose again, He completely stripped Satan of his power (Colossians 2 v 15) and made it inevitable that one day evil would be judged, punished and done away with for ever (Revelation 20 v 10).

After Jesus went back to heaven, He sent the Holy Spirit into the world to live inside all His followers. When Satan tries to get at Christians now, God is right there defending His children. So Satan can't force believers to disobey God; he can only encourage us to.

ENEMIES

That means we don't need to panic about evil in the world. And we don't need to get obsessed by it — it's far better to think about God than Satan! But there are things we can do to help ensure that we guard ourselves against Satan and don't get sucked into his plans (Ephesians 4 v 26–27). We can put on the armour of God! Chapter 6 of Paul's letter to the Ephesians makes it clear that the best defence against evil is to:

- believe what's true about God (v14)
- live in a right relationship with God (v14)
- share the gospel with others (v15)
- keep a strong faith (v16)
- be confident in Jesus' salvation (v17)
- know the Bible (v17)

And of course, we can turn to God in prayer too (v18). Dressed in these spiritual clothes and confident that God is in complete control, we can stand firm against anything Satan throws at us. And see him for the pathetic waster he really is!

43 | King of controversy

**We're back with Matthew's biography of Jesus.
How are you feeling? Calm? Excited? Worried? Bored?
Time for emotional aerobics now: this next controversial
story could leave you shouting: "That's not fair!"**

👁 Read Matthew 20 v 1–16

ENGAGE YOUR BRAIN

- ▶ *Does anything stick in your throat about this story?*
- ▶ *Is the landowner being unfair?*

Jesus said this story explained a truth about His kingdom (v1) — life with Him as King.

- ▶ *What do you think that truth is?*
- ▶ *Who's who in the story?*
- ▶ *So is God being unfair?*

God calls people to live under His rule and to work for Him (living His way, telling others about Jesus). And they get what God promised them — eternal life. And that's true, *whenever* they come to know Jesus. Awesome.

- ▶ *Did the last workers deserve a denarius?*
- ▶ *Did the first workers deserve to be hired?*

The landowner went back four times to hire new workers — that's how incredibly generous he was. It's ridiculous to be ungrateful and grumble at God for His compassion to others, when He's shown such amazing, undeserved love to us.

- ▶ *Does God give what He promises? (v13)*
- ▶ *Hasn't He the right to do as He wants? (v15)*
- ▶ *Is He generous to all His disciples? (v15)*

THE BOTTOM LINE

God's values are different from ours. This parable's a lesson in God's grace. So let's be thankful Christians working hard for Jesus, not grumbling grabbers after fame and status.

PRAY ABOUT IT

Thank God for His amazing grace. Pray that you'll grumble less at God and be more thankful.

➔ TAKE IT FURTHER

More controversy on page 116.

44 | Power serve

There's an old song about Jesus called "Meekness and majesty" — but the two don't seem to go together. How about "Meekness and being pathetic"? Or "Power and majesty"? But you can't mix the two, surely.

👁 **Read Matthew 20 v 17–19**

ENGAGE YOUR BRAIN

▶ What would have shocked the disciples about what Jesus said?

👁 **Read verses 20–23**

▶ What did James and John's mum ask for? (v21)

▶ How did Jesus answer? (v23)

"Can you drink from the cup I"m going to drink" means "Are you prepared to serve, suffer and be rejected as I will?" James and John said they were. And they did — both suffered loads as they spread the gospel. But only God the Father will decide who will have positions of honour in Jesus' kingdom.

👁 **Read verses 24–28**

▶ How did Gentile rulers act? (v25)

▶ How should believers be different? (v26–27)

▶ Why? (v28)

▶ Why did Jesus come into the world? (v28)

Greatness in the world's eyes is based on status, wealth and popularity. But greatness in God's kingdom is based on serving God and serving others. It's not about having power and bossing people around. It's about enduring hard times and injustice without complaining or turning away from God. True leaders should get their hands dirty with everyone else.

GET ON WITH IT

▶ How do you chase after status?

▶ How exactly will you be more of a servant this week?

→ **TAKE IT FURTHER**

Serving suggestions on page 116.

45 | Blind faith

Jesus and His disciples are on their way to Jerusalem, where Jesus has told them He will be tortured and killed. As they pass through Jericho, they're followed by a large crowd and are about to have a surprise interruption.

👁 Read Matthew 20 v 29–34

ENGAGE YOUR BRAIN

▶ Who shouted to Jesus?

▶ What did they call Him?

▶ What did they want?

▶ How did the crowd react?

▶ How did Jesus react?

▶ And what did the two men do then?

The crowd tried to silence these guys, but they shouted even louder to get Jesus' attention. They were blind, but could tell exactly who Jesus was. They called Him "Son of David". This is a name used in the Old Testament for the Christ — the King who would rescue God's people. They knew that Jesus was God's promised King.

And they knew He could heal them. Because they believed in Jesus, and because of His love for them, Jesus healed them. They followed Jesus.

THINK IT OVER

▶ Are you easily discouraged when people try to distract you from following Jesus?

▶ Are you determined to be a follower of Jesus?

▶ Do you truly believe that He's the King who can save you?

▶ Know anyone who's blind when it comes to Jesus?

▶ How can you follow Jesus more?

PRAY ABOUT IT

Use your answers to these questions to kick start your prayer time today.

→ TAKE IT FURTHER

Be blinded by more info on page 116.

46 | Royal visit

Donkeys. That's just the first surprise you'll get today. Jesus is on His way into Jerusalem, where His confrontation with those who refuse to accept His authority will continue. And boil over.

👁 **Read Matthew 21 v 1–5**

ENGAGE YOUR BRAIN

ⓘ *What were Jesus' weird instructions? (v1–3)*

ⓘ *Why did this happen? (v4–5)*

The Jews expected the Messiah to be a conquering hero arriving in style and force. But the Old Testament had promised that God's chosen Rescuer would be gentle and riding on a young donkey. Surprising.

👁 **Read verses 6–11**

ⓘ *How was Jesus greeted by the people? (v8–10)*

ⓘ *What did they recognise about Him? (v9)*

ⓘ *How did others describe Him? (v11)*

Jerusalem was packed with people ready to celebrate the Passover feast. They welcomed Jesus like royalty, praising Him. There was a huge buzz created by His entry — could this be the Messiah they'd been waiting for? Well, yes, He was! But Jesus wasn't the kind of King most people were expecting.

Hosanna means "Lord, save us". They were right that Jesus was their King who'd come to save them. But they thought He'd save them by fighting the Romans. They didn't realise that Jesus had come to die on the cross to save them from their sins. A few days later, another crowd would be shouting for Jesus to be killed!

PRAY ABOUT IT

Spend time praising King Jesus. Thank Him that He came as King to save His people from sin and punishment in hell.

THE BOTTOM LINE

Praise King Jesus! Welcome Him!

→ **TAKE IT FURTHER**

Visit Zechariah on page 116.

47 Tables turned

Jesus has arrived and is causing a big stir. He was doing loads of surprising stuff that fulfilled Old Testament prophecy about the Messiah. So people were amazed, yet many still refused to believe.

👁 Read Matthew 21 v 12–13

ENGAGE YOUR BRAIN

▷ *What surprising thing did Jesus do in the temple area?*

▷ *Why? (v13)*

He acted like it was His place. Actually, it was His Father's house and Jesus was furious with the way people abused it. The temple in Jerusalem was where people went to meet God. Instead of worshipping God, these guys used it to make money and scam people. They were also robbing God of the worship He should get in His house.

👁 Read verses 14–17

▷ *What kinds of people turned to Jesus? (v14–15)*

▷ *What about the religious leaders?*

▷ *How did Jesus answer them?*

Jesus was in Jerusalem, the city of God's chosen people. And everything He did pointed to His role as the promised one sent from God to rescue His people. Yet it was mostly outcasts and outsiders who realised who He was. Jesus was constantly showing from the Old Testament that He was the Christ, the Messiah. Yet the Scripture experts refused to believe it. Madness.

PRAY ABOUT IT

Pray that you won't make the same mistake as these leaders — knowing their Scripture, yet not getting to know Jesus. And pray that God will help you be accepting and encouraging towards believers who others look down on.

→ TAKE IT FURTHER

Psing a psalm on psage 117.

48 | Withering words

Jesus' actions in the temple had got up the noses of the Jewish leaders. How dare He call the shots in God's temple? Who does He think He is? Well, what happened next clearly showed what Jesus thought of them.

👁 Read Matthew 21 v 18–19

ENGAGE YOUR BRAIN
▶ What point do you think Jesus was making, bearing in mind what's happened in v1–17?

There's more than just a branch-withering miracle here. In the Old Testament, God described His people as a "fig tree". He expected "fruit" from them, or they'd be punished. People in Jerusalem were like this fig tree. They were very religious, with a reputation for serving God. But underneath, there was no real love for God. No fruit. One day, these people would be punished.

So what's this got to do with us? Well, we may do religious stuff, like going to church and not swearing much... but God sees what our hearts are really like.

👁 Read verses 20–22
▶ What were the disciples more interested in? (v20)

▶ What was Jesus' surprising news? (v21–22)

Anything is possible in God's power. If we truly believe that God can answer our prayers, then He will answer them. We've got to have faith.

PRAY ABOUT IT
Ask God to help you truly live like one of His children. And ask Him to help you really believe that He will answer your prayers.

➡ TAKE IT FURTHER
Words from Micah on page 117.

49 | Question time

Jesus was in Jerusalem and had fallen out with the Jewish leaders. He'd pointed out their hypocrisy and they didn't like the way He'd thrown people out of their temple. They were out to get Him.

👁 Read Matthew 21 v 23–27

ENGAGE YOUR BRAIN

▶ *What did they want to know? (v23)*

▶ *How did Jesus answer them? (v24–25)*

▶ *What was the problem? (v25–27)*

These ruthless leaders tried to trap Jesus. If He said: "God gives me this authority", they could arrest Him for blasphemy and sentence Him to death. And if Jesus said: "No one has given me authority to do this", He'd be shown up to be a big fraud. So Jesus asked them a trick question.

John the Baptist told people to get ready for Jesus, God's promised King. If these leaders said John's message came from God, they'd be admitting Jesus came from God too. But if they said it wasn't from God, they feared the crowds would turn against

them. So they refused to answer the question and so did Jesus.

👁 Read verse 28–32

▶ *What point did Jesus make with this story? (v31)*

Ouch! Jesus said corrupt cheats and prostitutes (who the religious leaders thought God would never accept) were being welcomed into God's kingdom. They'd seen the need to repent and trust. The religious leaders hadn't. So Jesus rejected them for rejecting Him — and turned to those who would accept and trust Him.

PRAY ABOUT IT

Rejecting Jesus outright is still a serious business. So is saying we follow Him and then doing nothing about it. Have you taken heart from the point of the story (v28–31)? Then talk to God about whatever's on your mind today.

➡ TAKE IT FURTHER

No *Take it further* today.

50 | Fruitless conversation

Jesus was challenged by the Jewish leaders to explain His authority. He refused point blank, saying God was rejecting them for rejecting Him. And He's not finished yet, using another story to trap them.

👁 Read Matthew 21 v 33–41

ENGAGE YOUR BRAIN

▶ *What did the owner want? (v34)*

▶ *But what did the tenants do? (v35–39)*

▶ *What did the Jewish leaders say should happen to the tenants? (v41)*

In the Old Testament, God spoke of Israel as His vineyard. So He's the landowner in this story. The tenants are religious leaders. The servants are God's prophets. The son is Jesus. So the story is a brief history of God's people, Israel. The leaders were outraged by what the tenants did, failing to realise that they were exactly like the tenants!

👁 Read verses 42–46

▶ *How did Jesus describe Himself? (v42)*

▶ *What would happen to Jewish people who rejected Jesus? (v43)*

▶ *How did the leaders react? (v45–46)*

God's people Israel, and its leaders, had rejected God's prophets down the centuries. And now they'd rejected God's own Son. So God turned to those who would accept Jesus as the world's ruler and would live lives that produced fruit for God. They would now be God's true people.

THINK IT OVER

It's easy for us to criticise these Jews for rejecting Jesus. But let's not miss the truth for us: rejecting Jesus is serious. And we reject Jesus when we think we know better than God and live our own way, not God's.

▶ *In what areas of life are you in danger of doing that?*
Talk it over with God right now.

→ TAKE IT FURTHER

Check out Isaiah on page 117.

51 | Wedding yells

Jesus told the religious leaders they were no longer God's people — because they rejected Jesus and failed to produce fruit for God. Here He rams home the point with another clever story.

👁 Read Matthew 21 v 1–7

This was the system: invitations were sent weeks in advance (and replies received). Then a second invitation (v3) was sent to inform guests when the banquet was ready. So the guests had already promised to come... and then didn't.

ENGAGE YOUR BRAIN

▷ *How did the guests respond to this second invitation? (v3–6)*

▷ *How did the king react? (v7)*

👁 Read verses 8–14

▷ *After rejection, what did the king do? (v8–10)*

▷ *Why was one guy thrown out? (v11–13)*

▷ *What's the message? (v14)*

The story's point was sharp — God was rejecting the nation of Israel for rejecting Him. So He was now turning to those who would accept Him and His invitation. But they'd need to live a changed life for the Lord. God wants people who keep going with Him. Christians who last. When God judges, they'll be recognised as His chosen people.

THINK IT OVER

▷ *Make a list of excuses people give for not keeping going with God:*

PRAY ABOUT IT

Pray for people you know who make those excuses (maybe yourself?), that they'll turn back to God. Thank Him for inviting you to His great heavenly feast. Pray that you'll remember this when life is tough, so you won't turn away from living for God.

➡ TAKE IT FURTHER

Feast yourself on page 118.

52 | Taxing question

The conflict between Jesus and the Jewish leaders had reached boiling point. They were furious and Jesus' claims that God would reject them for rejecting Him. They were out to get Jesus.

👁 **Read Matthew 22 v 15–22**

ENGAGE YOUR BRAIN

▷ Who did they enlist for help? (v16)

▷ How were they false? (v16)

▷ Why was their question (v17) a tricky one?

▷ How did He answer them?

▷ How did the trickster respond? (v22)

The Pharisees were Jewish leaders who hated their Roman rulers. The Herodians supported Herod, the local Roman ruler. The two groups would normally be enemies but the Pharisees were so desperate to get Jesus, they teamed up.

With this question, there was no way Jesus could please both sides. If Jesus said: "Yes, pay Caesar's taxes", the Pharisees could accuse Him of siding with the Romans against the Jews. If Jesus said "No", the Herodians could claim He was breaking Roman law.

Jesus' answer was perfect. It's right to pay taxes and obey the government's laws. But also there's a higher loyalty. Humans bear the image of God — and so must give God the obedience He deserves.

GET ON WITH IT

▷ In what ways do you disobey authority?

▷ In what specific ways can you give God what belongs to Him?
time:
money:
abilities:
your life:

PRAY ABOUT IT

Talk your answers over with God, committing yourself to doing them.

→ **TAKE IT FURTHER**

A tiny bit more on page 118.

53 | Seventh heaven

People were still chomping at the bit to try and trick Jesus. This time it was the Sadducees — a group of rich Jewish leaders. They didn't believe in resurrection — eternal life with God. And they were out to trap Jesus.

👁 Read Matthew 22 v 23–30

▶ How did the Sadd's try to trap Jesus?

▶ What was their problem? (v29)

▶ What had they failed to realise about life after death? (v30)

It doesn't seem very likely, does it? One woman marrying seven brothers, one after the other? The Sadducees thought this bizarre question would beat Jesus. They even quoted what Moses had said (v24). Surely Jesus couldn't get out of this one. But Jesus didn't waste much time with the Sadd' guys' question.

Of course eternal life won't be the same as this life. We'll have brand new bodies. And we won't be married — we'll be living with Jesus. The Bible tells us that marriage is a picture of the close relationship between Jesus and His people.

👁 Read verses 31–33

▶ What had the Sadd's failed to realise about God's people who had already died?

The Sadducees claimed there was no life after death. Yet God had said: "I **am** the God of Abraham, the God of Isaac and the God of Jacob" (Exodus 3 v 6). They'd been dead for ages, but God said He **is** their God. Abraham, Isaac and Jacob are alive and living with God in heaven!

SHARE IT

▶ As a Christian, what can you say to friends who claim there is no life after death?

▶ What can you tell them about the hope you have of eternal life?

PRAY ABOUT IT
Thank God for the great hope of a perfect future that Christians have, because of Jesus.

→ TAKE IT FURTHER
More about heavenly bodies on p118.

54 ¦ The greatest ¦

Yep, Jesus' enemies are still trying to trip Him up. What would you say is the greatest commandment in the Bible? And why would you argue that it's the most vital one?

👁 **Read Matthew 22 v 34–40**

ENGAGE YOUR BRAIN

▶ Who was out to get Jesus now? (v34)

▶ Why was this question so tricky?

▶ What's the most important command according to Jesus?

▶ And the second?

▶ Why are these commands so important? (v40)

The Pharisees were hoping to get Jesus to claim some parts of the Old Testament weren't so important. No chance. And again, Jesus' answer was brilliant. Give all of yourself to loving God. All your thoughts, words and actions should be for God! Christians still fail at times, but they really want to show their love for God. And part of the way we do this is by showing great love for people around us — not putting ourselves first all the time.

GET ON WITH IT

▶ If you take v37 seriously, what do you need to start doing?

▶ And stop doing?

▶ Write down the names of 6 people you see regularly — some you like and some you don't. Then write down a specific way you can show God's love to them.

1.
2.
3.
4.
5.
6.

PRAY ABOUT IT

Read verses 37–39 again and then look at your answers to *Get on with it*. You should now have loads to talk to God about!

➔ **TAKE IT FURTHER**

More commanding stuff on p118 .

55 | One last question

Over the last week, we've seen Jesus' enemies ganging together, asking Him ridiculous questions, trying to trap Him into slipping up. They failed miserably. So now Jesus has a difficult question for them.

Read Matthew 22 v 41–46

ENGAGE YOUR BRAIN

▶ What was His question and how did they answer it? (v41–42)

▶ How does Jesus use Scripture to baffle them? (v43–45)

▶ How did these Old Testament experts respond? (v46)

In Jesus' time, Jewish people were waiting for the Christ to rescue them. The Pharisees knew that the Christ would be related to King David (v42). So they thought he was a man, and couldn't be God as well!

Verse 44 is something King David wrote in Psalm 110. By calling the Christ my Lord, David is saying that the Christ is also God. The Jewish leaders hadn't worked this out. But we know that Jesus is the Christ, who rescues His people. And that He is God too!

Jesus had been called "Son of David", so they knew He was challenging them to accept Him as the Christ. They refused to, and next time they met, it would be to arrest Him.

THINK IT OVER

People still offer every excuse and argument possible to avoid accepting Jesus as King. Do you make that mistake too?

PRAY ABOUT IT

Thank God that Jesus is the Christ — the perfect King who God sent to rescue us from the punishment we deserve for our sins. Ask God to help you get the message of Jesus across to those who refuse to believe. And pray that you'll live in a way that shows Jesus is King of your life.

→ TAKE IT FURTHER

No *Take it further* today.

56 | Horrible history

Psalm 105 was a lesson in God's faithfulness. And a prompt to shout about it. This next psalm shows how amazing it is that God acted like that. Look how His people treated Him.

👁 **Read Psalm 106 v 1–5**

ENGAGE YOUR BRAIN

▶ *What should God's people do? (v1)*
▶ *Why? (v1–2)*
▶ *What else should they do? (v3)*

👁 **Read verses 6–33**

▶ *How had God's people sinned? (v7)*
▶ *Yet what did God do? (v8–11)*
▶ *Why? (v8)*
▶ *How did the Israelites respond? (v12)*
▶ *But then what? (v13–14)*
▶ *So what did God do? (v15–18)*
▶ *How would you describe the pattern of behaviour shown by the Israelites and God?*

👁 **Read verses 34–48**

▶ *What other terrible things did God's people do? (v34–39)*
▶ *How did this make God feel? (v40)*
▶ *So what did He do? (v41–43)*
▶ *Yet how did He show His enduring love? (v44–46)*
▶ *What responses should all this stir up in God's people? (v47–48)*

THINK IT OVER

This psalm is about the sin of the Israelites in Old Testament times — and God's punishment and incredible love. Jot down why this psalm is still hugely relevant in the 21st century.

PRAY ABOUT IT

God's faithfulness is all the more remarkable in the light of the way we treat God. Think what's right and good to say to God now. And do it.

➔ **TAKE IT FURTHER**

Write your own psalm! On page 119.

TOOLBOX

Which Bible?

One of the main ambitions of **engage** is to encourage you to dive into God's word and learn how to handle it and understand it more. Each issue, TOOLBOX gives you tips, tools and advice for wrestling with the Bible. This issue, we look at different versions of the Bible.

There are so many different translations of the Bible available, it's difficult to know which one to choose. Do you stick with an older "reliable" version like the NIV or New King James, or do you try something newer? Or are you more swayed by Bibles that look good or have the word YOUTH emblazoned on them? Where do you start?

WORD FOR WORD

The Old Testament was written in Hebrew (with a few bits in Aramaic), and the New Testament was written in Greek. Some English versions translate these ancient versions very literally, word for word. This means what we read is very close to what the original Hebrew or Greek is saying. But the resulting English can sometimes be difficult to read or sound weird.

For example, a literal translation of Genesis 4 v 1 is: *"Now Adam knew Eve his wife, and she conceived and bore Cain"* (ESV). It sounds strange. Obviously Adam *knew* his wife — it would be a weird marriage if they'd never been introduced! The thing is, to "know" in Hebrew is a polite way of talking about having sex. That makes much more sense! Adam had sex with Eve and she conceived and gave birth to Cain. But the literal translation keeps the exact Hebrew expression that's hard to understand.

THOUGHT FOR THOUGHT

Other versions translate idea for idea ("dynamic equivalence"), resulting in translations that are easier to understand, but not so close to the actual wording of the original. So sometimes they help the flow of the writing by adding in words that aren't

in the original at all, and that can be potentially unhelpful.

MIX AND MATCH

The way to avoid errors like this is to check what you're reading against more than one translation. So if you're using a thought for thought translation, it's handy to have literal translation too.

At the more literal end of the spectrum are NASV, and ESV and NKJV. At the more "readable" end, are the CEV and NCV and New Living Translation. The popular NIV is somewhere in the middle. There are also *paraphrases*, which simplify or expand the author's words to make the Bible easier to understand. *The Message* is the best known example of a paraphrase.

If you ever want to compare different Bible translations, check out www. biblegateway.com. Pick out some favourite verses in advance so you can compare them in different versions.

DO IT YOURSELF

Read Ephesians 5 v 18 in the NIV (use www.biblegateway.com if you need to).

▶ *What do you think being "filled with the Spirit" is about?*

▶ *How do you know? Where did you get your definition from?*

Read Ephesians 5 v 18–21 in the ESV or NKJV (more literal translations).

▶ *Can you see how v18 is connected to what follows?*

▶ *What four things does Paul associate with being filled with the Holy Spirit?*

▶ *How does this compare with your definition of a Spirit-filled person?*

Ideas taken from Dig Deeper by Nigel Beynon and Andrew Sach. Published by IVP and available from The Good Book Company website.

57 ¦ 2 Kings: Decline and fall

Back to the soap opera of 2 Kings. So far, we've met a lot of bad kings in Israel and Judah. But now Joash, king of Judah, and his people are turning back to God. But how long will it last?

👁 Read 2 Kings 12 v 1–3

ENGAGE YOUR BRAIN

▷ *How did Joash behave, at first? (v2)*

▷ *What didn't he do? (v3)*

👁 Read verses 4–16

▷ *What did Joash want to do? (v5)*

▷ *How successful was he? (v6)*

▷ *What did Joash do about it? (v7–12)*

Things were going well. King Joash repaired God's temple. The priests were slow getting around to it, but it finally happened. Great news! But...

👁 Read verses 17–21

▷ *What happened? (v17)*

▷ *How did Joash deal with the threat? (v18)*

▷ *Who did this treasure really belong to?*

▷ *What eventually happened to Joash? (v20)*

Joash's time as king started so well!

But as soon as he was threatened, he buckled. He bribed the king of Aram with treasures from God's temple, instead of turning to God for safety and protection. The book of 2 Chronicles mentions even worse stuff that happened during Joash's reign.

GET ON WITH IT

▷ *If things are going well with you, what might mess up your relationship with God?*

▷ *What can you do to stop this happening?*

▷ *If things are going badly, what do you need to do?*

▷ *What can you ask God?*

Talk to God openly about this stuff.

→ TAKE IT FURTHER

More about Joash on page 119.

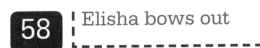

58 | Elisha bows out

We're moving from Judah to Israel now. It's been ages since we heard from Elisha. It's time for one last impressive story from his life. As usual, the kings of Israel are messing things up.

👁 Read 2 Kings 13 v 1–9

ENGAGE YOUR BRAIN

▶ How is King Jehoahaz summed up? (v2)

▶ How was God closely involved with His people? (v3–5)

▶ Yet how did they treat God? (v6)

When we see God's love and mercy, it should affect us so powerfully that we change our sinful ways.

👁 Read verses 10–19

▶ How is Jehoash described? (v11)

▶ Yet how did he react when he heard Elisha was dying? (v14)

▶ What did Elisha tell the king to do? (v15–18)

▶ What was the outcome of his half-hearted efforts? (v19)

God promised to help Jehoash and the Israelites defeat the Arameans. Jehoash should have grasped this promise confidently. But he didn't seem to fully trust God and so they didn't fully destroy their enemies.

▶ When are you half-hearted about trusting or serving God?

👁 Read verses 20–25

▶ How was Elisha involved in a miracle even after his death?

▶ Despite their sin, how did God treat His people? (v23)

God is so loving and compassionate to His people. Even when they disobey Him, He always keeps His promises (v23–25).

GET ON WITH IT

▶ How will remembering God's love and mercy spur you on to change your ways?

→ TAKE IT FURTHER

Find the dead body on page 119.

71

59 Slide rule

Israel was still on the slide. In these next chapters, king after king gets dismissed with the line: "He did evil in the eyes of the Lord". It's a nation heading for judgment. But Judah still seemed to be trying to live God's way.

👁 Read 2 Kings 14 v 1–22

ENGAGE YOUR BRAIN

- ▶ How would you describe King Amaziah of Judah? (v3–4)
- ▶ What did he do right? (v5–7)
- ▶ What did he get wrong? (v8–12)
- ▶ What happened to Jerusalem, God's city? (v13–14)
- ▶ And to Amaziah? (v19)

Let's move from Judah back to Israel.

👁 Read verses 23–28

- ▶ How successful was Jeroboam II? (v25, 28)
- ▶ But what was the verdict on him? (v24)
- ▶ Even so, how did God use him? (v26–27)

👁 Read 2 Kings 15 v 8–31

- ▶ What did these kings of Israel have in common? (v9, 18, 28)
- ▶ What else? (v10, 14, 30)
- ▶ How did God keep His promise? (v12)

👁 Read 15 v 1–7, 32–38

- ▶ How did the kings of Judah differ from the kings of Israel? (3, 34)
- ▶ But what did they get wrong? (v4, 35)

Things were starting to fall apart for God's people in Israel and Judah. Israel turned away from God and would soon be punished for it. Judah was mostly living God's way but not as wholeheartedly as they should. The future wasn't bright. If you ignore God and reject His ways, eventually everything will fall apart. His judgment must be faced.

PRAY ABOUT IT

Thank God for His faithfulness even when we ignore Him. Pray that you will do what's right in His eyes.

→ TAKE IT FURTHER

Slide on over to page 119.

60 | The tide turns

In recent chapters, Israel's kings have all been bad — doing evil and rejecting God. Judah's kings haven't been perfect, but they've mostly served God. Sadly, that was about to change.

👁 **Read 2 Kings 16 v 1–9**

ENGAGE YOUR BRAIN

▶ How bad was King Ahaz? (v2–4)

▶ What trouble was Ahaz and Israel in? (v5)

▶ So what did Ahaz do? (v7–9)

Ahaz turned away from the God-serving ways of his ancestors and worshipped false gods. And in panic he turned not to God, but to evil superpower Assyria. He even gave the king of Assyria treasures from God's temple. This was a sad day in Judah's history. It would now be a servant-state of Assyria.

👁 **Read verses 10–20**

▶ Why did Ahaz build an altar? (v10)

▶ What was he doing wrong? (see Hebrews 9 v 1)

▶ But who was Ahaz's "god"? (v18)

Oh dear. Ahaz adopted Assyria's religion, and brought its ways back into God's temple in God's city, Jerusalem. Disgusting. Judah was now in Assyria's pocket and Ahab was a puppet king. Depressing. But all was not lost for Judah. Find out why in two days.

THINK IT OVER

▶ When things get tough, what do you do?

▶ Who should you turn to?

▶ Who gets more of your "worship" and time than God does?

PRAY ABOUT IT

Turn to God now with anything that's worrying you at the moment. Pray that you'll put Him first, not letting other relationships become more important to you.

➔ **TAKE IT FURTHER**

Words from Isaiah on page 119.

61 | The end for Israel

The final curtain was about to be drawn. The axe was poised. The final whistle would be blown. Whichever way you put it, it was zero hour for Israel. God had had enough of His own people spitting in His face.

👁 Read 2 Kings 17 v 1–23

ENGAGE YOUR BRAIN

▶ What's the verdict on Israel's last king? (v2)
▶ What did he do instead of trusting God? (v3–4)
▶ What happened and why? (v5–7)
▶ Why could they not blame God? (v13–17)

Verses 7–8 sum up centuries of Israel's history:
a) they rejected God and chose to worship idols.
b) they behaved like the nations around them.
c) Israel's kings even introduced new, godless ways.

God warned them and gave them time to repent. But Israel's stubborn rebellion brought God's judgment crashing down on the nation.

👁 Read verses 24–41

▶ What was the problem in Samaria? (v25)

▶ What great thing happened? (v28)
▶ What was the problem with their worship? (v33)
▶ Why was this so bad? (v35)
▶ What does God expect from people? (v35)

God won't share praise with anything else. Why should He? He created us and demands our loyalty, love and devotion. We can't be like the people of Samaria, devoting ourselves to God AND other things — He must be number one.

GET ON WITH IT

▶ What or who does God have to share your devotion with?
▶ How can you make God number one in your life?

THE BOTTOM LINE

"Do not worship any other gods."

→ TAKE IT FURTHER

A little more on page 120.

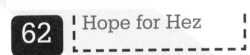

62 | Hope for Hez

The northern kingdom of God's people, Israel, was now over. They'd refused to turn back to God, so He let the Assyrians obliterate them. But Judah's time wasn't up yet. Step forward King Hezekiah.

Read 2 Kings 18 v 1–8

ENGAGE YOUR BRAIN

▷ How was Hez different? (v3–6)
▷ What resulted? (v7–8)

Read verses 9–37

▷ What was the bad news for Hez and Judah? (v13)
▷ How did Hez keep peace for a while? (v14–16)
▷ How did the Assyrians scare God's people?
  v21:
  v22:
  v25:
  v27:
  v33:

Read 2 Kings 19 v 1–19

▷ What was Hez's hope? (v4)
▷ How did Isaiah encourage him? (v6–7)
▷ How did the king of Assyria respond? (v9–13)
▷ What did Hez pray? (v15–19)

God would again care for His people as they trusted Him (as He'd said in His covenant). If only God's kings and God's people had done so more often before this point. But Sennacharib hadn't finished pumping out threats to God's people. He sent a letter to Hez, who turned to God for help. He knew God created everything — only the Lord could save Judah from the terrifying might of the Assyrians.

PRAY ABOUT IT

▷ What tips can you take from Hez's prayer for when life seems hard?

Follow Hez's example and bring your worries and concerns before God now, remembering how powerful He is. Tomorrow, we'll discover what happened.

THE BOTTOM LINE

God is faithful to His people and nothing is impossible for Him.

→ TAKE IT FURTHER

More hope on page 120.

63 Roots of recovery

The story so far: Good King Hez is in charge of Judah. But Judah is being threatened by Sennacherib, king of Assyria, who has already wiped out Israel. Hez cried out to God for help. But how would God respond?

👁 Read 2 Kings 19 v 20–28

▶ *What comfort did Isaiah give Hez? (v20)*

▶ *What big mistake had Sennacherib made? (v22–23)*

▶ *But who had given Senna his power? (v25)*

▶ *What would happen to Senna and why? (v28)*

👁 Read verses 29–37

▶ *What did God promise Hez?*
v29:
v30–31:
v32–34:

▶ *What happened? (v35–37)*

The Assyrians had devastated Judah's land and crops. The people would have two more years without much food, but then God would give them a good harvest (v29). Much better than that, God promised to stop the Assyrian invasion and destroy Sennacherib. And even better than that, out of tiny, nearly defeated Judah, great things would come (v30–31). Ultimately, that would mean Jesus. All of this would happen — God promised it and showed great zeal (enthusiasm) to save His people.

In this life, things often look bleak for God's people. Sinful people seem to be successful, while many Christians are downtrodden and (in many parts of the world) persecuted. But God will protect His people and one day there will be a great harvest. Evil will be punished and God's people will live in perfection eternally.

PRAY ABOUT IT

Thank God for His great promises and that the future is bright for His people. Pray that you will remember this when life looks bleak.

→ TAKE IT FURTHER

More on page 120.

64 | Good news bad news

Do you sometimes live as if you're two different people? There's the "holy" you, who lives for God, and does and says the right things. And there's the side of you who doesn't trust God fully, and makes bad choices. King Hez was a bit like that too.

👁 **Read 2 Kings 20 v 1–11**

ENGAGE YOUR BRAIN

▶ What was the bad news? (v1)

▶ What kind of king had He been? (v3)

▶ What great news did God have for Hez? (v5–6)

▶ Why did God do this? (v6)

▶ What sign did God give Hez? (v11)

Hez was staring death in the face. He told God how he felt and how he'd served the Lord. God heard his prayer and gave Hez 15 more years of life, and He used Isaiah to heal Hez. God proved He'd keep His word by making the shadows move the opposite way to normal. God is so compassionate to His people. He hears our prayers.

👁 **Read verses 12–21**

▶ Where were the visitors from? (v12)

▶ What did Hez do? (v13)

▶ What was Isaiah's chilly message? (v16–18)

▶ How did Hez take the news? (v19)

Hez was a perfect host to his guests from Babylon. But now this distant superpower knew about Judah's wealth, strengths and weaknesses. Isaiah told Hez that Babylon would one day take everything. It seems Hez wanted to rely on powerful "friends" for security, not just the Lord. And Judah would pay the price.

PRAY ABOUT IT

Ask God to help you trust Him fully. To rely on Him alone and not fall for flattery from His enemies.

→ **TAKE IT FURTHER**

More from Hez on page 121.

65 | Man monster

Any idea which king of God's people reigned the longest? David? Solomon? Actually, it was Manasseh. So, he must have been the most loyal, God-serving king, right? Wrong. He was one of the most depraved of the lot.

👁 Read 2 Kings 21 v 1–9

ENGAGE YOUR BRAIN

▶ *What was so bad about Manasseh? (v2–6)*

▶ *What was the privilege and responsibility of God's people? (v7–8)*

▶ *But how did they act? (v9)*

Criminal: in the exact place where God shared His presence with His people, Manasseh set up an idol (v7). Manasseh's rule was a bad influence on God's people (v9). They became worse than the godless nations God had already wiped out around them!

👁 Read verses 10–26

▶ *How would God punish Judah? (v12–14)*

▶ *Why? (v15)*

▶ *What was Manasseh's son Amon like? (v20–22)*

God had been patient with His disobedient people for so long. But Judah was living on borrowed time. God's people had failed for centuries to keep God's covenant. Manasseh was the worst of them all and the last straw. God had declared His judgment. It was only a matter of when.

THINK IT OVER

▶ *What should be our ongoing response to this God?*

▶ *How seriously should we treat the sin in our lives?*

▶ *Why?*

PRAY ABOUT IT

Spend time admitting your recent sins to God. Be honest, open and repentant. Ask Him to help you fight the sins you struggle with. Commit yourself to living for Him.

→ TAKE IT FURTHER

Could Manasseh change? Page 121.

66 | Raiders of the lost book

Judah was a nation with God's judgment hanging over it. Let's find out how the next king handled things.

👁 Read 2 Kings 22 v 1–13

ENGAGE YOUR BRAIN

- ▶ How careful was young Josiah to follow God? (v2)
- ▶ What did he send his secretary to do? (v4–6)
- ▶ What had the priest found? (v8)
- ▶ What effect did God's book have on King Josiah? (v11)
- ▶ Why? (v13)

Maybe it was Deuteronomy they found, or a slice of it. Either way, it laid down God's covenant. And the consequences of disobeying it.

👁 Read verses 14–20

- ▶ What was the message from God? (v16–17)
- ▶ What was the good news for Josiah? (v19–20)

After reading God's law, Josiah realised the people of Judah had turned away from God and would be punished. He turned to God's prophetess for help. The bad news was that God would still punish Judah for all its hideous sins against Him. But God would show mercy — He would hold off His judgment until after good king Josiah was long gone.

God's word is often not easy to swallow. It can cause distress, show our sin and require big changes. Josiah's response was the right one — saddened by sin, but willing to accept God's punishment and to ask Him how to make things right.

PRAY ABOUT IT

Think how you can be more like Josiah as you talk to God right now. Perhaps God's showing you areas in your life that need to be dealt with. Talk to Him about that.

THE BOTTOM LINE

Gods' word should affect us deeply.

→ TAKE IT FURTHER

Meet Zephaniah on page 121.

67 | Read and learn

King Josiah has discovered the book of God's law which highlighted how Judah had turned away from Him. They deserved God's punishment. Let's see exactly how God's people should react to His word.

👁 Read 2 Kings 23 v 1–30

1. COMMIT TO GOD
▶ *What did Josiah make everyone do? (v1–2)*
▶ *How did everyone respond? (v3)*

First off, we must read God's word, listen to it, learn from it. And then commit ourselves to obeying it and living God's way.

2. DITCH BAD STUFF
▶ *What did Josiah do with anything to do with idol worship? (v4–14)*

If God's word challenges us that we've been disobeying Him, then we must kick out all the stuff in our lives that tempts us to sin.

3. REMEMBER GOD'S PROMISES
In destroying these idols and idol-worship areas, Josiah was fulfilling God's promises from years before (v15–18). God always keeps His promises — both for His people and against His enemies.

4. DO WHAT IT SAYS
▶ *What did Josiah command? (v21–23, 24–25)*
▶ *Why? (end of v21, end of v25)*

Josiah took God's words very seriously. He followed them and committed his whole life to obeying them. Josiah's reign was successful. Sadly, it was too little too late and God would still punish His consistently disobedient people.

GET ON WITH IT
1. Will you commit yourself to living God's way?
2. What will you kick out of your life so you can serve God better?
3. Which of God's promises do you need to remember?
4. Which of God's commands will you take more seriously?

Talk through these four steps with God, working out exactly what you'll do. Ask for His help.

→ TAKE IT FURTHER
Josiah extra on page 121.

68 | The end?

God's promise to punish rebellious Judah came true. Next, in just 22 years, Judah had four kings and Jerusalem got invaded three times.

👁 Read 2 Kings 23 v 31 – 24 v 7

ENGAGE YOUR BRAIN

▷ *What was good king Josiah's son like? (v32)*
▷ *What happened to him? (v34)*
▷ *What was the effect on Judah? (v35)*
▷ *What about Jehoiakim? (v37)*
▷ *Who was behind the attacks on Judah? (24 v 2)*
▷ *Why? (v3–4)*
▷ *Who was the new superpower? (v7)*

👁 Read 24 v 8–17

▷ *What was Jehoiachin like? (v9)*
▷ *What happened during his reign? (v13, 14–15, 16)*

The beginning of the end for Judah. Only farmhands left — anyone who might organise trouble was taken away (v14)

👁 Read 24 v 18 – 25 v 30

▷ *What happened to Judah and why? (24 v 20)*

Jerusalem's leaders were killed, the city trashed and the temple (the sign of God being with His people) torched. Any who joined Zed's revolt against Neb were beheaded (v21). God's people were taken away from their country.

Then we're told (v27–30) Judah's last king, Jehoiachin, was freed from prison in Babylon. After 37 years. So what? Well, God had promised not to wipe out the line of King David. The story of God and His people, despite this shattering judgment, would continue.

PRAY ABOUT IT

We're left waiting at the end of 2 Kings for a leader who can really sort out God's people. We're waiting for God to send His Son to rule as King on earth. Thank God for all you've learned from 2 Kings. And praise Him for Jesus, the perfect King.

→ TAKE IT FURTHER

Not quite the end... try page 121.

Non-Christian family

Everyone's family is different. In character, closeness, complicatedness… and Christian-ness. Maybe you're reading this because you have a non-Christian parent or a relative who has a go at you for what you believe — you're facing aggression at home. Maybe you're reading because you've got a non-Christian family member you wish would at least ask you what you believe — you're facing apathy at home.

Most of us will have a family member who doesn't share our view on life and death, heaven and hell, and who Jesus is. That can be a source of great sadness to us. But it shouldn't be a surprise to us, because:

1. IT'S PART OF THE CHRISTIAN LIFE

Jesus said this is how life would be: *"Do you think I came to bring peace on earth? No, I tell you, but division. From now on there will be five in one family divided against each other, three against two and two against three"* (Luke 12 v 51–52).

We can't sit on the fence as far as Jesus is concerned. In our hearts, we're either loving Him, or disliking Him. When those two attitudes exist within the same family, it causes division.

2. IT WAS PART OF JESUS' LIFE

Not long after Jesus had started teaching and healing, his family decided: *"He is out of his mind"* (Mark 3 v 21). Even Jesus' family at one stage thought He was crazy! If that's how some of your family treat you because you're a Christian, talk to Jesus about it. He knows exactly how you feel.

BUT WHAT CAN I DO?

Despite opposition, it's great to be a Christian — to know God loves you, to know what life's all about, to look forward to perfection with Jesus beyond death. And you'll want your

whole family to know all that too! Whether your family are aggressive or apathetic, what can you do to get them to take Jesus seriously?

Four tips:

*"**OBEY YOUR PARENTS** in the Lord, for this is right"* (Ephesians 6 v 1). This is hard. It's unfashionable. But it's what God wants, and will show your parents that actually Christian faith strengthens family life, rather than breaks it up. (Notice, though, we're to obey them *"in the Lord"* — what God says comes first. If a parent tells you to stop praying, or not think about Jesus anymore, you'll need to politely refuse.)

PRAY FOR YOUR FAMILY

Paul prayed for all his distant relatives, the whole nation of Israel — we should at least pray for our immediate family! Don't just pray that they'll be happy or healthy; pray they'll come to trust Jesus. As Paul put it: *"My heart's desire and prayer to God for the Israelites is that they may be saved"* (Romans 10 v 1).

SHOW THEM CHRIST.

"Live such good lives among the pagans (ie: non-Christians) *that … they may see your good deeds and glorify God"* (1 Peter 2 v 12). If you want your family to take Christianity seriously, you need to show them that it's worth taking seriously — that it makes a difference.

TELL THEM ABOUT CHRIST.

"Always be prepared to give an answer to everyone who asks you to give the reason for the hope that you have" (1 Peter 3 v 15). If your family see you living differently, they'll ask you why. Be prepared to take a risk and tell them it's because of Jesus.

BUT IT'S NOT WORKING!

Often, because we so desperately want those we love to be saved, we get disheartened if they don't become Christians in a week, or a month, or a year. Stick at it. It takes some people decades before they're ready to take Jesus seriously — but at that moment, wouldn't it be great if you were there for them? Praying for them. Showing them Jesus in how you live. And ready to talk to them about Jesus and how great it is to be part of His family.

69 | JUDE: Fight for the faith

Jude is a little letter. Just 25 top quality verses. It's written by Jude (no surprise), who's the brother of James. That's James who wrote the book of, er, James. So Jude's also the brother of Jesus.

Jude has just caught a whiff of a massive danger to the church. It's so subtle it's creeping in almost unnoticed, but it's so dangerous it's threatening to lead Christians away from Jesus and even to rob them of eternal life.

Jude gives a load of powerful examples to warn us about dangerous people, some of them leaders, who try to drag God's people down. And Jude tells us clearly how to rescue people — ourselves and others — from their threat. Fight for the faith, he says. Stick by the gospel. Your eternal life depends on it.

But first, Jude's introduction.

👁 Read Jude v 1–2

ENGAGE YOUR BRAIN
▷ *How does Jude describe himself?*

▷ *How does he describe the Christians he's writing to?*

▷ *Why is that encouraging?*

Those who trust Jesus have been called by God, they're loved by Him and are kept for the future by Him. Christians can say God has brought us to Himself, hasn't let us go and never will. Jude wanted his readers to be sure of that, especially as this new threat could shake their faith.

SHARE IT
▷ *How can you remind Christian friends of the great truths of v1?*

▷ *Will you do it right now?*

PRAY ABOUT IT
Thank God that Christians are called by Him, loved by Him and kept by Jesus Christ. Now pray verse 2 for believers you know.

→ TAKE IT FURTHER
More info on Jude on page 122.

70 | Gospel gate-crashers

Ever gate-crashed a party? You're not really invited, but thought you'd slip in unnoticed. Jude talks about church gate-crashers. They slipped in unnoticed among the Christians and were trying to rip the church apart.

👁 Read Jude v 3–4

ENGAGE YOUR BRAIN

▶ *How does Jude describe these gate-crashers? (v4)*

▶ *What did they change about the Christian message?*

▶ *How did Jude want his readers to respond? (v3)*

Think this danger isn't really a threat to us? Think again. Have you ever thought: "I'll do whatever I like — God will forgive me"? Or: "What you believe about Jesus isn't that vital"? In v5–16, Jude fired off loads of examples to explain the consequences of living with wrong attitudes to God and to the gospel of Jesus.

THINK IT OVER

▶ *When you hear teaching about Jesus that's wrong, do you:*
a) not notice?
b) ignore it?
c) find a way to question?

👁 Read verses 5–7

▶ *What 3 examples does Jude give?*

▶ *How is each of them like the gate-crashers in v4?*

▶ *What happened to them?*
v5:
v6:
v7:

Each had great privileges, but didn't trust God or live His way. Those "godless men" of v4 could expect the same destiny. In fact anyone who knows God's love and yet turns against Him can expect God's furious punishment when Jesus returns.

PRAY ABOUT IT

Pray that you'll recognise false teaching when you hear it. Pray that your church / youth group won't be sidetracked by false teaching or sin.

→ TAKE IT FURTHER

Follow the Roman road to page 122.

85

71 ⟦ Strong words ⟧

Christians often hold back from saying what they really mean. They can water down their words so as not to offend anyone. But Jude doesn't. He uses lots of inventive language to say exactly what he thinks of these bad guys.

👁 Read Jude v 8–11

ENGAGE YOUR BRAIN

▶ What does Jude call these men in v8?

▶ How did they live? (v8)

▶ What was their conversation like? (v10)

▶ What else did they do and what would be the consequence? (v11)

Jude doesn't mince his words! They rejected authority, sinned sexually, talked offensively about stuff they didn't understand and were murderously greedy. But God would deal with them. He never leaves sin unpunished.

👁 Read verses 12–16

▶ What do you think Jude means when he calls these men…
greedy shepherds?
clouds without rain?
fruitless, uprooted autumn trees?
wild waves, foaming with shame?
wandering stars in the darkness?

▶ How else are they described? (v16)

▶ What did Enoch say would happen to them? (v14–15)

These guys grumble; they're never satisfied; they go back on any initial commitment to Christ; they pump up themselves and others to ensure they're popular. They clearly haven't submitted to God or trusted Jesus' rescue. The end was inevitable for them — God would punish them. But how do we stand up to people who try to destroy the church? Jude will tell us tomorrow.

PRAY ABOUT IT

Ask God to help you know when you're being persuaded by wrong attitudes or poor teaching. Thank God that He rightly punishes such people. And pray that He'll throw out anyone like that from your local churches.

→ TAKE IT FURTHER

Tackle the tricky bits on page 122.

72 Fighting talk

Jude switches from danger to response. From "why" to "how". Chew on his jam-packed sandwich — two slices of reminders (v17–19, 24–25), with an oozy filling of instruction (v20–23).

👁 **Read Jude v 17–19**

ENGAGE YOUR BRAIN

▷ *How would v17–18 both encourage and warn readers?*

▷ *What did they need to remember? (v19)*

These men twisted the gospel and wouldn't accept Jesus — they didn't have God's Spirit. They were involved in church, but weren't Christians.

👁 **Read verses 20–23**

▷ *What should Christians do?*

-
-
-
-
-
-

GET ON WITH IT

▷ *How will you build up yourself and others in the faith?*

Keeping ourselves in God's love (v21)

will involve obeying Him. Think of your attitude to: Christians caught in two minds (v23a); those living blatantly ungodly lives (v23b). What will you do?

Notice the warning — watch it, or you'll get sucked into joining the behaviour of ungodly people too.

👁 **Read verses 24–25**

▷ *What great truths does Jude remind us about?*

▷ *How do v24–25 encourage you?*

▷ *Is your view of God as big as this?*

PRAY ABOUT IT

Write down what you'll remember from reading the mostly unknown letter of Jude. And also what changes you'll make. Talk to God about these things and ask Him to help you fight for the faith.

➔ **TAKE IT FURTHER**

The last word on Jude — page 122.

87

73 | Alternative love song

It's time for a song. It's a long one and it's all about God's enduring love for His people. It's not wishy-washy love — it's love that speaks through action, mercy and sometimes discipline. Listen in to this love song.

◉ Skim read Psalm 107 v 1–32

ENGAGE YOUR BRAIN

▷ *What examples of God's love are we shown?*
v4–9:
v10–16:
v17–22:
v23–32:

▷ *What happened each time? (v6, 13, 19, 28)*

▷ *What was the result? (v7, 14, 20, 29–30)*

▷ *What's the right response? (v1, 8, 15, 21–22, 32)*

Some of God's people experienced hardship and hostility (v4–5); some brought themselves into captivity by disobeying God (v10–11); some made their lives miserable by rebellious ways (v17); others found danger in life's ordinary activities. But when they cried out to God for help, He rescued them. What incredible love.

◉ Read verses 33–43

It's a reminder that God's people messed up — turning away from Him many times. Verses 34 and 40 remind us that God acts quickly to punish rebellion. One day He'll do that decisively, and finally, for all people.

But God didn't abandon His people. Time after time He intervened to rescue them.

▷ *What are you learning about God's love?*

▷ *How much is He in control of all circumstances?*

PRAY ABOUT IT

This is a song for us too — God's people rescued by Jesus' death. Thank God that He's no pushover. Thank Him that He's chosen to stand by and care for His people.

→ TAKE IT FURTHER

No *Take it further* today.

74 | Cry of victory

Take a slab from Psalm 57 and another from Psalm 60, mix them together and you get Psalm 108. It's a corker — full of great reminders about our incredible God.

⊙ **Read Psalm 108 v 1–5**

ENGAGE YOUR BRAIN

▶ What's David doing? (v1–3)

▶ Why? (v4)

▶ What's his great desire? (v5)

⊙ **Read verses 6–13**

▶ What situation does David look back on? (v11)

▶ What does he ask God for now? (v6, 12)

David is confident of God's help against his enemies — wading in to fight back at the Edomites (v10, 13).

▶ What is it that gives David such confidence? (v7–9)

David remembers God's promise (to give land to His people and to defeat their enemies) and prays about it.

▶ How might this change the way

you pray?

This psalm also points us to Jesus — the King of God's people who'd defeat the enemy and rescue His people. Just as God promised.

THINK IT OVER

Think how Jesus revealed the depth of God's love and faithfulness. And think how our hearts can be steadfast (v1). It's when we recall God's character and claim His promises.

▶ What are you trusting in each day? What will you trust from now on?

PRAY ABOUT IT

Thank God that He cares about your situation when things are tough, but also thank Him that He is in control of it, however bad things seem.

→ **TAKE IT FURTHER**

A tiny bit more... on page 123.

75 ¦ 2 Corinthians continued

Let's dig back into Paul's difficult letter to the Christians in Corinth. Paul has been given an amazing job by God and he wants the Corinthians to understand that, understand him and stand with him in it.

👁 Read 2 Corinthians 6 v 3–13

ENGAGE YOUR BRAIN

▶ What is Paul concerned about in verse 3?

▶ What has he gone through for the sake of Christ? (v4–5)

▶ How does he behave? (v6–7)

▶ What extremes has he experienced? (v8–10)

▶ Why can he (and we) rejoice even in sorrow?

▶ How can he/we make others rich?

▶ How do we possess everything even if we are materially poor?

The Christian life can be really tough. It can involve serous suffering and persecution. Yet despite that, we can rejoice in knowing God, in having our sins forgiven, in having a wonderful inheritance secure in heaven and in being "in Christ" — everything is ours. And we can share those riches with others!

PRAY ABOUT IT

Thank God for all that is yours in Christ and ask Him for opportunities to share that treasure with your friends and family.

▶ What does Paul want most of all from the Corinthians (v11–13)?

It's a direct, personal, heart-felt appeal to the Corinthians. Would they remain loyal to him, God's apostle?

THE BOTTOM LINE

You might have nothing, but in Christ you possess everything.

TAKE IT FURTHER

Continue continuing on page 123.

76 Continuation situation

Ever left a red sock in with a white load of washing? When you open the washing machine door, everything has turned pink and your dad is not pleased that his white work shirt is now a delicate rose colour. Some things can't help contaminating what's around them.

👁 **Read 2 Cor 6 v 14 – 7 v 1**

ENGAGE YOUR BRAIN

▶ What does Paul warn the Corinthians about in v14?

▶ Why is he so concerned about it? (7 v 1)

▶ What illustrations does Paul give of things that cannot go together. What makes them so incompatible? (NB Belial = the devil)

▶ How are Christians described? (v16)

▶ What does that mean? (v16)

PRAY ABOUT IT

How amazing is it that God is living in you by His Spirit? Thank Him for His love towards you and His promise in verse 18.

GET ON WITH IT

Is there any way that you are currently "yoked with unbelievers"? Paul doesn't mean that we should have nothing to do with non-Christians, or how would we ever get to share the gospel with them?

He's talking about close relationships (like cattle "yoked" together to plough fields!) where we are likely to be contaminated by ungodly ideas and dragged away from Jesus. This is one major reason why it's a bad idea to start dating someone who doesn't believe in Jesus.

THE BOTTOM LINE

Do not be yoked with unbelievers.

→ **TAKE IT FURTHER**

The yokes on you — page 123.

77 Joy ride

Paul had sent Titus with a strongly worded letter to Corinth, and he was waiting anxiously to see how it had been received (2 v 13). Well, now Paul is put out of his misery and gets the lowdown from Titus...

👁 Read 2 Corinthians 7 v 2–16

ENGAGE YOUR BRAIN

▶ *How does Paul feel about these Christians? (v3)*

▶ *How was Paul feeling when he arrived in Macedonia? Why? (v5)*

▶ *What changed that? (v6–7)*

▶ *How had the Corinthians responded to Paul's hard words? (v8–11)*

▶ *How do you respond when someone points out your sin?*

▶ *What about when God points it out when you read His word?*

PRAY ABOUT IT

Read verse 10 again. Feeling sorry for our sin is great if it leads us to repent, to turn back to God and take our sin back to the cross. Feeling guilty and miserable but refusing to change is pointless and will not get us anywhere. Talk to God now about your sin.

ENGAGE YOUR BRAIN

▶ *Paul is delighted that the Corinthians have turned back to God. Why else is he happy? (v13–16)*

▶ *Have you ever recommended a film or book that you really love to someone? How do you feel when they love it too?*

Paul really cares about this church; he was as embarrassingly proud of them as a granny getting photos out of her purse to show everyone.

THE BOTTOM LINE

Godly sorrow leads to repentance.

➔ TAKE IT FURTHER

Happy happy joy joy on page 123.

78 Give give give

We all like to be on the receiving end of generosity. But when you hear someone churn out the old saying: "It's better to give than to receive" do you agree?

👁 **Read 2 Corinthians 8 v 1–5**

ENGAGE YOUR BRAIN

▶ *What is the Macedonian churches' attitude towards giving to the poor in Jerusalem? (v1–5)*

▶ *What motivated their generosity? (v2)*

▶ *Did their giving depend on what they could spare? (v3)*

How would you define generosity? What is the difference between putting your spare change in a collecting tin and deciding to go without something so you can use the money for God's work?

👁 **Read verses 6–15**

▶ *What was the Corinthian attitude towards giving? (v10)*

▶ *How does Paul encourage them? (v6–8, 11–12)*

▶ *How should Christian generosity work? (13–15)*

Marxism is famous for the saying: "From each according to his ability, to each according to his need". But that's actually a Bible principle!

▶ *Who is the greatest giver of all (v9)?*

▶ *How rich was Jesus?*

▶ *How poor did He become?*

▶ *How rich are we?*

PRAY ABOUT IT

Thank Jesus for verse 9. Praise God for His grace — His undeserved kindness to us.

GET ON WITH IT

Do you need to review the way you give your time, talents and money? Make definite plans and then stick to them.

THE BOTTOM LINE

Jesus was rich but became poor so that we could be rich.

→ **TAKE IT FURTHER**

Give more on page 123.

79 Give and let give

Have you ever boasted about how good you are at something, only to attempt it and fall flat on your face?

👁 Read 2 Cor 8 v 16 – 9 v 5

ENGAGE YOUR BRAIN

- ▶ What do Paul and Titus share? (v16)
- ▶ How has Paul chosen the men who will administer this gift for the poor? (v18–23)
- ▶ How would you describe Paul's methods? (v20–21)
- ▶ Why might giving from one set of Christians to another be so controversial?

The early church was made up of a mixture of Jews and non-Jews. It took time for people to overcome their prejudices against each other. Jewish Christians (like those in need in Jerusalem) might have been too proud to accept help from those they considered beneath them (the non-Jewish Corinthians).

TALK IT OVER

Chat with another Christian about how you respond when someone offers to help you. Do you find it easy or difficult to accept other people's generosity? Why do you think people find it hard to accept help, especially money, when they are struggling?

- ▶ What has Paul boasted about (v2)?
- ▶ What is he worried about? (v4–5)
- ▶ What is the difference between a generous gift and one grudgingly given?
- ▶ Which would you rather receive?
- ▶ Which brings more glory to God?

PRAY ABOUT IT

Ask God for a generous heart and for the grace to receive help graciously and humbly.

THE BOTTOM LINE

Let us give generously and receive graciously.

→ TAKE IT FURTHER

Receive more on page 123.

80  Gleeful giving

God loves a cheerful giver. Ever heard that said? Well, this is where it comes from!

👁 **Read 2 Corinthians 9 v 6–11**

ENGAGE YOUR BRAIN

▶ *What is the logic of v6? Why should we give generously?*

▶ *How should we approach giving our time, talents and money? (v7)*

▶ *Are you a cheerful giver?*

▶ *Who is the most generous giver of all? Hint: look back at 8 v 9!*

▶ *How does God act towards us? (v8–11)*

Notice in verse 8 that God's grace to us abounds or overflows so that we can then abound in every good work.

▶ *When we give away, in what way do we gain more than we give? (v10)*

▶ *What is the end result of giving generously? Is it so people think we're great? (v11)*

Our giving, like our whole lives, should result in praise and thanksgiving towards God. Our purpose is to bring God glory.

PRAY ABOUT IT
Thank God for all He has given you and all He continues to give you. Ask Him to help you remember that and to respond with thanksgiving towards Him and with generosity to others.

TALK IT OVER
Chat about v7 with another Christian. How does that affect how you might respond to someone collecting for charity on the street or a TV fundraising show? Is it better to proactively decide what you want to give money to or react to need? Or should we do both?

THE BOTTOM LINE
God's grace towards us overflows!

→ **TAKE IT FURTHER**
More about giving on page 124.

81 | Think thanks

Do you write thank-you letters for presents you've received? Even though it can seem like a chore, it's good to give thanks to the source of the good things we receive.

⬤ Read 2 Corinthians 9 v 12–15

ENGAGE YOUR BRAIN

▶ What two effects do the Corinthians' generosity have? (v12)

▶ What two effects will their generosity have on people who hear about it? (v13–14)

▶ What effect does it have on Paul? (v15)

▶ What is God's indescribable gift?

God is so generous to us in Christ; He also enables us to respond in thanksgiving and generosity towards others. Other Christians are helped and thank God. Others hear and praise God.

▶ Who is the focus on throughout this "cycle of giving"?

PRAY ABOUT IT

Thank and praise God now, who gives us all good things and, best of all, gave us His Son.

▶ What do you do to remember how generous God is?

▶ How should thinking about all He's given us affect the way we pray?

▶ How about when we're tempted to sin?

▶ Or when we need His forgiveness for messing up yet again?

THE BOTTOM LINE

Thanks be to God for His indescribable gift!

TAKE IT FURTHER

A little more on page 124.

82 | Choose your weapons

Paul returns to the tricky issue of his opponents and their criticisms of him. They claim that despite his bold letters, he is really nothing to worry about in person. They're about to discover Paul's no pushover!

👁 **Read 2 Corinthians 10 v 1–18**

ENGAGE YOUR BRAIN

▶ How was Paul criticised? (v10)

▶ Who does Paul imitate? (v1)

▶ What will Paul be "bold" in dealing with? (v2, v5–6)

▶ Who is behind Paul? (v4, 13)

▶ What is Paul's God-given task? (v13–16)

When people attack us, it's very easy to spend time and energy defending and justifying ourselves. Paul gives a brief explanation of why he is as he is, but his main focus is on God, who has given him a task and enabled him to do it.

▶ What do we learn about Paul's opponents? (v12, 15–16)

The non-Christian world is very good at slander, gossip and spreading unsubstantiated rumours. Our "weapons" should be very different. The gospel is God's power — only the message of God's truth can change the pride and unbelief in people's minds. And it announces Jesus' demand on every area of life, especially our thinking (v5).

PRAY ABOUT IT

Pray for God's wisdom (see James 3 v 17), and God's strength (see Ephesians 6 v 10–18), when you face opposition.

THE BOTTOM LINE

Do not live by the standards of this world.

→ **TAKE IT FURTHER**

Under attack on page 124.

83 ¦ Fraud squad

Accused of being ordinary, Paul replied that his weapon — the gospel — could bring even the proud to submit to Christ. Accused of being an idiot and weak, Paul let fly.

👁 Read 2 Corinthians 11 v 1–6

ENGAGE YOUR BRAIN

▶ What is Paul concerned about? (v1–3)

▶ What have these new teachers been doing? (v4)

▶ How have the Corinthians responded?

▶ How do these new teachers see themselves? (v5)

One criticism being made of Paul was that he worked for free. Clearly, these super-apostles considered themselves to be worthy of large pay packets and implied that anyone who worked for free, like Paul, was inferior.

TALK IT OVER

What do you think Paul would say to church leaders who demand large salaries and drive expensive cars as a sign of their worth?

👁 Read verses 7–15

▶ How did Paul live while he was sharing Christ with the Corinthians? (8–9)

▶ What motivated him? (11–12)

▶ Why are these false teachers so dangerous (v13–15)?

▶ What will their fate be?

PRAY ABOUT IT

Pray that you would never be led astray (v4) and that God would help you to remain devoted to Christ (v2–3).

THE BOTTOM LINE

Remain sincerely devoted to Christ.

→ TAKE IT FURTHER

A tiny bit more on page 124.

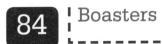

84 | Boasters |

In case they still haven't got the message about why Paul is to be trusted and listened to, Paul decides to highlight how foolish his opponents' bragging and boasting is. Here Paul uses sarcasm to devastating effect.

◉ Read 2 Cor 11 v 16–33

ENGAGE YOUR BRAIN

▷ Are the Corinthians as wise as they think? (v19–21)

▷ What are the false teachers really like? (v20)

▷ Is Paul's "weakness" really that shameful? (v21)

▷ How does he beat his opponents at their own game? (v22–29)

▷ Why do you think Paul only wants to boast of his weakness? (v30–33)

▷ Who gets the glory?

All of Paul's sufferings show how amazing and powerful God is, who kept him alive, and enabled him to continue sharing the gospel. The Corinthians were too easily impressed by boastful, "successful" people. They had forgotten they were following a Lord who died in shame on a cross.

PRAY ABOUT IT

Read 1 Corinthians 1 v 18–31 and thank God for His "foolishness" and "weakness" that is far greater than all our human wisdom and strength.

GET ON WITH IT

When you talk about what God is doing in your life, does the glory go to you or Him? It's very easy to impress other Christians with our achievements, holiness and even humility. Get your focus right — any progress we make is entirely down to God's grace.

THE BOTTOM LINE

To God be the glory.

→ TAKE IT FURTHER

Thought-provoking stuff on page 124.

85 | Thorny issues

Ever heard the term "thorn in my flesh" or "thorn in my side"? We're not talking about a nasty cactus incident, by the way...

👁 Read 2 Corinthians 12 v 1–6

ENGAGE YOUR BRAIN

▶ *What will Paul boast about and what won't he boast about? (v5)*

It seems a funny way of writing it, but Paul is probably talking about himself in verses 2–4. But notice that despite this amazing experience, he only wants the focus to be on his weakness so that God's strength can be shown.

👁 Read verses 7–10

▶ *How did God help Paul to stay humble and dependent on Him? (v7)*

▶ *What did Paul ask for? (v8)*

▶ *What was God's response and why?*

We don't know what Paul's "thorn" was. It might have been bad health, a particular temptation, persecution or maybe even the false teachers,

but that's not important.

▶ *Where did the "thorn" come from? (v7)*

▶ *Who was really in control? (v9)*

▶ *When bad or annoying things happen, do you trust that God is behind all events for your good?*

▶ *How should we pray in those sorts of situations?*

▶ *How did Jesus pray? (Matthew 26 v 36–45)*

PRAY ABOUT IT

Spend some time thinking about the difficulties in your life. Ask God to transform the way you look at them so that you can depend more and more on His strength when you feel weakest.

→ TAKE IT FURTHER

Brilliant Bible bit on page 124.

86 | Follow the leader

Paul has been hurt by the way the Corinthians believed and even passed on the accusations of his opponents, these so-called "super apostles". He shouldn't have to explain himself; they should know what he's really like.

👁 Read 2 Cor 12 v 11–18

ENGAGE YOUR BRAIN

▶ *What accusations have been made against Paul? (v11, 16)*

▶ *How does he reject them? (v12, 17–18)*

Paul plans to visit the Corinthians for a third time, and once again he doesn't want their money but their hearts.

▶ *What is his true attitude towards the Corinthians? (v13–15)*

▶ *What about Titus? (v18)*

▶ *Can you see the same attitude in your Christian leaders?*

▶ *Do you have that attitude towards your fellow Christians?*

▶ *Where does Paul's attitude come from? (clue: Philippians 2 v 1–11)*

PRAY ABOUT IT

Ask God to give you the same concern to serve others that Paul had, not thinking about your own gain but wanting the best for others. Ask Him to help your church leaders to have that kind of heart also.

THE BOTTOM LINE

Let your attitude be the same as that of Christ Jesus...

→ TAKE IT FURTHER

Follow the leader to page 124.

101

87 | Worried words

Things are all building up to Paul's next visit now as he prepares to finish his letter. What's on his heart as he gets ready to sign off?

👁 Read 2 Cor 12 v 19–21

ENGAGE YOUR BRAIN

▶ What has Paul been doing in these last couple of chapters according to verse 19?

▶ Who is Paul's judge?

▶ What is Paul's concern?

Verse 20 says that Paul is afraid that the Corinthians will not be as he wants them to be — pure and devoted to Christ. And he's also worried that they won't find him as they would want him to be — criticising their wrongdoing rather than encouraged by their faith and full of joy.

PRAY ABOUT IT

Do you cause joy or grief to your leaders — whether at church, youth group or even your parents? Are you as they (and Christ) would want you to be? Talk to God about it now.

▶ What is Paul worried he might find in the Corinthian church? (v20)

▶ What would upset him? (v21)

Notice that it's not just the sin that makes Paul sad; it's the lack of repentance. We all get things wrong from time to time, even Christians! But a true Christian is sorry for their sin, desperately wants God's forgiveness and turns away from their wrongdoing with the help of God's Holy Spirit.

THE BOTTOM LINE

The Christian life involves repenting and believing on a daily basis.

→ TAKE IT FURTHER

Get some more on page 124.

88 ⌐ Testing times ⌐

Once again, Paul tries to prepare the Corinthian church for his third visit. The last one wasn't a roaring success and despite some pretty strong letters, Paul longs for things to be different.

👁 Read 2 Corinthians 13 v 1–4

ENGAGE YOUR BRAIN

▶ What is Paul concerned he will discover in Corinth? (v1–2)

▶ What sort of "sin" might he be talking about? (look back to 12 v 21)

▶ What is God's attitude to sin?

▶ And Paul's? (v2–3)

The Corinthian church had got the idea that Paul was weak, but as he points out in verses 3–4, he's only as weak as the God he serves. Jesus may have died in "weakness" but was raised in power and it is by the same power that Paul speaks and acts.

👁 Read verses 5–10

▶ How are the Corinthians to "test" that they are truly in the faith? (v7)

▶ Does this mean that true Christians never do anything wrong?

Remember 12 v 21. The genuine Christian always repents. Paul is worried that there are some people calling themselves Christians who are shamelessly carrying on in serious sin.

▶ What is Paul's prayer for the Corinthian church? (v9)

▶ How does he want to use his God-given authority as an apostle? (v10)

▶ How could he use it?

PRAY ABOUT IT

Are you taking sin as seriously as God does? It led Jesus to the cross. Talk to Him now about any thoughts, words or actions you need to repent of.

THE BOTTOM LINE

We are weak, but in Christ we are strong.

→ TAKE IT FURTHER

Test yourself from page 125.

89 See ya later!

It's been a pretty tough letter in many ways — dealing with false accusations, trying to put the church back on the right track, tackling the sensitive issue of money and helping the Corinthians to see suffering the right way. How will Paul end his letter?

👁 Read 2 Cor 13 v 11–14

ENGAGE YOUR BRAIN

▶ What does Paul call these guys? (v11)

▶ What is Paul's final appeal to them? (v11)

▶ What promise does he give them? (v11)

▶ How will that help them to do what they need to do?

Despite all the controversy and difficulties, Paul wants these Christians to live in harmony with each other and with all Christians. The holy kiss bit just means be affectionate towards each other; you don't necessarily have to go round kissing every Christian you meet!

Verse 14 has become a famous blessing which people often say at the end of Christian meetings.

▶ Why are the three things in v14 so important for the Corinthians and all Christians to have?

PRAY ABOUT IT

Notice that Paul calls the Corinthians brothers (and sisters); they are part of a worldwide family, and so are we. Spend some time now praying for Christians you know (or even ones you don't) in other parts of the country or world. Why not use verse 14 to help you?

THE BOTTOM LINE

Grace, love and fellowship. We need all three.

→ TAKE IT FURTHER

The last word on 2 Corinthians is on page 125.

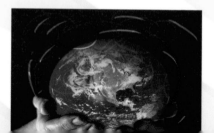

90 | Angry words

Here's a screamer of a psalm. David's had it tough, been betrayed nastily by a friend, and now wants God to punish his enemy. The bluntness of this psalm is shocking. Just see what David prays...

👁 **Read Psalm 109 v 1–5**

ENGAGE YOUR BRAIN

▷ What's happened to David?
▷ What makes it so unfair?

👁 **Read verses 6–20**

▷ What does David want?
  v6–7:
  v8:
  v9–10:
  v11:
  v13–15:
▷ Why does David feel so strongly? (v16–20)

What an outrageous ouburst! Hideous, murderous, ferocious. David's asking God to wipe out this man's life, family, business, descendants, and any memory of him.

👁 **Read verses 21–31**

▷ How does David feel? (v22–25)
▷ What does he ask God to do? (v21, 26)
▷ Why is he still able to praise God? (v30–31)

Should we echo David's words against *our* enemies? Against our human enemies — no. Check out **Romans 12 v 17–21**. Use the gospel to "fight" these enemies. If they trust in Christ, they will no longer be our enemies.

We also have spiritual enemies (Ephesians 6 v 12). This is where we can echo David's prayer. And we can share his confidence that God will save us from these enemies. Like David, we should want justice — evil to be punished and God to be honoured. And we should be confident that God will carry out His promises.

PRAY ABOUT IT

Talk to God about people who treat you badly. He's in control and will judge everyone fairly in the end. Pray that you won't take revenge. Ask Him to work in the hearts of your enemies so they're transformed by Jesus.

→ **TAKE IT FURTHER**

More on this psalm on page 125.

91 | Judge, Priest and King

Here's a psalm by David that has deep, deep, er, depth. We've already seen Jesus quote part of it when we were reading Matthew's Gospel. So guess who it points us to.

👁 Read Psalm 110 v 1–3

ENGAGE YOUR BRAIN

▷ What will God do for the person David's singing about?
v1:
v2:
v3:

The New Testament quotes this psalm loads, saying it's about Jesus. About His return to God's presence after being raised from the dead. On the cross, Jesus defeated all His enemies — and will finally dispose of them on the day He returns as Judge.

👁 Read verses 4–7

▷ What has God promised Jesus? (v4)

▷ What will Jesus do, and when? (v5–6)

▷ How is His humanity shown? (v7)

Melchizadek (v4) was a king and priest who blessed Abraham. Here,

he symbolises what Jesus would do — He'd both rule the world and open the way back to God. Permanently.

He will also return one day as Judge, to punish those who've rejected God. Judge. Priest. King.

PRAY ABOUT IT
Use this psalm to help you thank God for Jesus — what He has done and what He will do.

→ TAKE IT FURTHER
Take it further, one last time, over on page 125.

TAKE IT FURTHER

If you want a little more at the end of each day's study, this is where you come. The TAKE IT FURTHER sections give you something extra. They look at some of the issues covered in the day's study, pose deeper questions, and point you to the big picture of the whole Bible.

MATTHEW
King of controversy

1 – BLIND FAITH
Read verse 2 again

"Tradition of the elders" — rules passed down from generation to generation. The Pharisees' biggest mistake was making these manmade rules equal in authority to God's laws in the Old Testament.

Read verse 19

Jesus isn't saying we can't be creative, logical etc. He's saying that when it comes to being good enough for God, our hearts are totally messed up. We need new hearts. The heart of the human problem is the problem of the human heart. But Jesus came to fix that problem.

2 – GONE TO THE DOGS
Read Matthew 28 v 18–20

- ▶ *How much power does Jesus have? (v28)*
- ▶ *So what does He command His followers to do? (v19–20)*
- ▶ *And what great promise does*

He make?
- ▶ *So what does all this mean for Christians like us?*

3 – SIGN LANGUAGE
Read Matthew 12 v 38–41

Jonah's ordeal showed God's rescue and grace to him personally. But Jesus' death and resurrection showed God's grace and rescue to the **whole world**.

The people of Nineveh were going to be forgiven and given hope because Jonah preached to them. This could only happen because he'd been in the big fish for three days. Jesus spending three days in the earth (between His death and resurrection) ultimately gives us the chance of forgiveness, and hope for the future.

Check out **1 Peter 1 v 3–4**; then thank God for what Jesus' death and resurrection means for you.

4 – STALE BREAD

The disciples' double mistake was
a) failing to trust Jesus for food
b) failing to grasp His teaching. >>>>

ⓓ How carefully do you listen to Bible teaching?

ⓓ What teaching that's around at the moment do we need to guard against?

When listening to or reading books by Bible teachers, we must be on our guard, not just blindly accept everything we're told. Ask: Do they believe that...

a) Jesus was both God and man
b) God is a trinity
c) what the Bible teaches is 100% true
d) people are sinful
e) Jesus' death is the only way to make us right with God

Don't hold back — ask questions! Check what you hear with what the Bible says. And ask older Christians you trust.

5 – JESUS JIGSAW

Read verse 19 again

Here's how Michael Green explains it: "The power to bind and loose ... meant to allow or disallow conduct, based on God's laws in the Old Testament. Jesus came to fulfil God's Old Testament law and gave Peter the responsibility of interpreting Jesus' teaching for others. This responsibility would also be given to the rest of the disciples (Matthew 18 v 18).

"Peter was also given *"the keys of the kingdom of heaven"*. He and the disciples were given the responsibility of sharing the gospel and therefore making God's kingdom accessible to everyone who

heard their message. If people respond to the conditions of the gospel — repent and believe — they can be assured that God has forgiven them. If they refuse to repent and believe in Jesus, they won't receive forgiveness from God."

6 – CROSS WORDS

Read verse 28 again

It's hard to tell if Jesus is referring to the transfiguration (that comes next) or the resurrection, or Pentecost or the telling of the good news of Jesus. Any ideas?

Using v13–28, imagine explaining to a non-Christian friend:

a) who Jesus is
b) what He came to do
c) what response He demands

Why not practice what you'd say?

7 – MOUNTAIN TENSION

Read verses 1–3 again

In the Old Testament, Moses went up a mountain to meet God (Exodus 24). And so did Elijah (1 Kings 19 v 8–18). Moses and Elijah represented the law and the prophets of Israel. Here they met Jesus, who'd come to fulfil what both the law and prophets had looked forward to.

8 – DEMON DISARRAY

Read verse 20 again

There's not much that's smaller than a mustard seed, so these guys must have shown no faith at all! It's not the amount of faith that's important — even the smallest is enough. What matters is who we put our faith in. God can do anything. OK, so we probably won't need literally to move any mountains, but God can achieve the seemingly impossible through us, if we trust Him to.

10 – WHO'S THE GREATEST?

Read verse 4 again
Then Philippians 2 v 5–11,
focussing on v8

▶ *Who is Jesus? (v6)*
▶ *What didn't He do? (v6)*
▶ *What did He do? (v7–8)*
▶ *What did God think of this? (v9)*

Jesus is worth it — He's God! But He gave up everything He deserved and was humble enough to die on a Roman cross to serve others.

▶ *So what does that mean for us? (v5)*

Here's our motto for life — not *because I'm worth it* but *my attitude should be the same as that of Christ Jesus*. We live Jesus Christ's way by copying His attitude.

11 – CUT IT OUT

▶ *How serious are you about stuff that causes you to sin?*
▶ *And about what you do (or fail to do) that makes others sin?*
▶ *Need to make an action plan?*
▶ *Need to ask an older Christian to keep an eye on you?*

12 – CLASHING CHRISTIANS

Read verses 15–16 again
When another Christian offends us,

we should go and see them in person. Texts, emails, letters and even phone calls are a less personal form of communication. Face to face is best. We shouldn't dread such confrontation: after all, we're all accepted by God. And He will help us sort out our differences.

13 – DON'T FORGET TO FORGIVE

Read Genesis 4 v 24
Just as Lamech's revenge was unlimited, so should our forgiveness be.

▶ *What evidence is there in your life that you know God's forgiveness?*
▶ *Do you care for others' relationship with God?*
▶ *Are you quick to apologise to others?*
▶ *Do you forgive?*
▶ *Need to ask God's help?*

14 – THE D-WORD

Read Matthew 19 v 13–15
Jesus' views on marriage and divorce were controversial. And so was what He said about children. Kids were seen and not heard, and were definitely looked down on. So the disciples trying to get rid of the kids hanging around Jesus was just what people did back then. But Jesus didn't like that attitude. Children matter, and have much to teach us. Their trust, simplicity and dependence are all things Christians should show in their relationship with God and with other believers.

15 – MONEY TALKS

Read verses 17–20 again
The man fails to see he'll never be able to

keep God's commandments. And he fails to recognise who Jesus is: if he'd done so, surely he'd have done whatever it takes to follow Jesus.

Read verse 21

Is this a demand for every Christian? Well, we'd all like to answer "No" and say it's just for the rich who love money. But Jesus doesn't allow such sidesteps — following Him means turning our back on anything we've previously set our hearts on.

▶ *What's that for you?*

16 – MISSION POSSIBLE

Read verses 28–30 again

Those who follow Jesus are the "true Israel" — God's true people. Israel the nation rejected Jesus and killed Him. They were the first to have a chance at eternity with God, but many of them turned away from God. And those who have given up everything to follow Jesus will find many surprises waiting for them in eternity!

2 KINGS
Decline and fall

17 – FLAMING FIREBALLS!

Does Elijah's action (v10, 12) seem unfair and unjustified? Does it put God in a bad light?

▶ *What clues are there in this chapter that this wasn't personal revenge, but a demonstration of God's justice?*

Read verses 3–4 again

God shows He won't share His supremacy with any other.

▶ *Why's it important that we remember God is jealous and wants our complete commitment?*

▶ *What are some of the ways we're tempted to worship other things as well as God?*

▶ *In what ways do you do that?*

19 – DIRTY WATER AND BEAR ATTACKS

Read Galatians 6 v 7–10

▶ *What's the message for people who mock God? (v7)*

▶ *What happens if we chase our sinful desires? (v8)*

▶ *What's the good news if we live to please God? (v8)*

▶ *So what should we do? (v9–10)*

▶ *How exactly will you do that this week?*

20 – THREE KINGS

Read verses 26–27 again

King Mesha of Moab is in desperate trouble. To get out of it, he attempts to break through enemy lines with a crack unit of 700 soldiers (v26). He fails. Even more desperately, he then sacrifices his son (heir to the throne) to the god Chemosh. He succeeds. But why does Mesha's sacrifice seem to work?

Well it's not entirely obvious. But it can't be that Chemosh was responding to the child sacrifice as he was a fake god — utterly powerless. Only the Lord has power to intervene in wars. So it seems as though God was disgusted with Israel's sin and refused to give them complete victory.

The Israelites were supposedly God's people, yet they were worshipping false gods, just like the king of Moab! Idiots. They were turning from the true, powerful, gracious God and turning towards false gods and idols. This could only ever lead to defeat and horrible sin (such as child sacrifice). Turning *from* God always means turning *to* something far worse.

21 – MORE 'MAZING MIRACLES
Read verses 27–33
We've seen how impressive and powerful Elisha was. Look at all the miracles he did! But these verses show him lacking knowledge (v27) and power (v29–31). The only thing he could do was rely fully on God — turning to Him in prayer. Elisha wasn't the impressive one. It was all down to God. We should remember this whenever we look up to other Christians. We should celebrate what God does through them. But we shouldn't idolise them — it's always God who's behind it.

22 – FANTASTIC FOOD PHENOMENA
We've seen some incredible miracles in 2 Kings 4. God was dramatically highlighting Elisha as His spokesman. But...
• would the kings of God's people pay attention to him?
• would they turn back to God and obey Him?

The miracles showed God's power and His willingness to care for His people. And, at this time when godless kings led Israel and Judah away from God, the miracles were pointers to the need to listen urgently to what God said. Take the hint?

23 – A CLEAN START
Read verses 17–19
Naaman probably thought that God could only be worshipped on Israelite soil. He was going to take loads of soil back home so he could worship God there. But the Lord can be worshipped anywhere. Naaman had not understood that fact, but the more important fact was that he now wanted to worship God! Brilliant.

In verse 18, it says that as part of his job, he must go with the king when he worships the false god Rimmon. Naaman seems to be saying that he himself won't be worshipping Rimmon — he'll worship God from now on. But he can't really avoid going to Rimmon's temple with his boss. Elisha sent Naaman away in peace and didn't seem offended by this, perhaps because Naaman was far closer to God than many Israelites! This doesn't mean we can worship other things as well as God. But it does show that sometimes our work and our friends put pressure on our loyalty to God. Like Naaman, it's good to talk these things over with other believers.

24 – AXE OF KINDNESS
Read verses 18–23

The blindness here probably isn't total loss of sight but more like confusion. Elisha led them on a 10-mile walk to Samaria! The king of Israel wanted to kill the enemy but Elisha persuaded him to be kind to them and he gave them a feast before sending them home. Unusual. What do you think the Arameans felt about it all? They'd fallen into the enemy's hands and God's prophet had spared them.

When God opened their eyes and they realised they were in front of the King of Israel, they must have been terrified and expecting death. They were spared. Hopefully they realised that God had protected them and spared them. In this story, God not only protected His servant (Elisha) and His people (Israel), but also the enemy (Aram)! God's love, care and protection is on offer to anyone!

26 – MORE BAD KINGS
Read verses 1–6 again

God showed great kindness to this woman. Elisha acted as a famine early warning system, so she was able to move away before the hard times came. But while she was away, someone nabbed her land. When she goes to the king to beg for her land back, Gehazi just happens to be talking about her — more great timing from God. The king could see for himself the boy that God (through Elisha) had brought back to life.

After hearing all about God's grace, the king responds in the right way by showing grace and generosity to the woman and her family.

▶ *How have you seen God's grace and generosity?*
▶ *So who can you show such generosity and kindness to?*
▶ *What will you do?*

27 – HIRED HITMAN
Read verses 30–37 again

What a strange story! When Jezebel heard Jehu was on his way to kill her, she put her best make-up on so she looked all queenly. When Jehu arrived in his chariot, she accused him of being like Zimri, who had seized the throne from King Elah, 45 years earlier (1 Kings 16 v 8–20). Zimri destroyed Elah's whole family, and that's what Jehu had in store for Ahab's family.

Jehu persuaded a couple of eunuchs (castrated males, working for Jezebel) to throw her out of the window to her death. Despite all the blood, Jehu went inside for lunch. After calming down a bit, he gave orders to have Jezebel buried — after all, she was royalty. The problem was, there was hardly anything to bury. Dogs had eaten her up, just as God's prophet, Elijah, had predicted years earlier (1 Kings 21 v 23).

28 – HEADS WILL ROLL
Read verse 11 and then Hosea 1 v 4

Jehu, it seems, went beyond God's instructions, killing more than necessary.

He was more interested in personal advancement than obeying God, and he took no steps to reform Israel.

29 – KID FOR KING

Read verses 17–18 again, then Luke 14 v 25–33

▶ *If you're considering becoming a Christian... what's Jesus telling you to do first? (v28–30)*

▶ *If you're already a Christian... what's Jesus telling you following Him will be like? (v27)*

Jesus isn't saying hate your relatives. He's saying you can't follow Him halfheartedly. Either He's your number one, and you're willing to suffer for Him, or you're not. Either you're a 100% follower, or you're no follower.

Following Jesus is like running a marathon; it's the finishing that counts, not the starting. Before you start, you must decide to keep going to the finish even when it hurts. Same with following Christ! Still, it's better to be on Jesus' side than opposing Him, like it's better for a king to be at peace with a stronger king instead of getting slaughtered by him (v31–32).

2 CORINTHIANS
Power in weakness

30 – COMFORT ZONE

Read verses 3–7

▶ *How does the God of all comfort actually comfort us and then others?*

v4:

v6:

v7:

2 Corinthians 7 v 6–7:

▶ *How can you comfort people you know who are suffering?*

▶ *How can you share Christ's comfort with them?*

31 – YES MAN

Read verses 19–20, then Luke 24 v 27

When you read the Old Testament, do you do it wearing "Jesus glasses"? There are some great video clips on the web with summaries of how Jesus fulfils the Old Testament. Why not hunt some down?

32 – FORGIVENESS

Someone once said: "*A Christian leader needs to be ice-cool, rarely open with their emotions and a little distant*". Rubbish! Find verses in today's passage which show Paul was the exact opposite. Now pray for Christian leaders you know.

Forgiveness is something that the world finds very hard to do.

▶ *Why do you think that is?*

▶ *What difference does being a Christian make?*

33 – SMELL OF SUCCESS

Read 2 Corinthians 3 v 3–6 again

Why is Paul using this image of stone tablets? The main focus of these intruders' teaching was the Old Testament law given through Moses. But Paul points out here that the law simply highlights our sin without giving the solution (v6). When Jesus came, He both fulfilled the law's requirements AND gave us His Spirit by which we could live (v3 & 6). This new covenant brought His Spirit to change people's hearts and enable them to live for Him. Miles better than Moses.

34 – GLORY STORY

The Old Testament contains many "trailers" for Jesus Christ, but the reality is far better. Check out **Hebrews 12 v 18–24** and give thanks.

35 – SEE THE LIGHT

Verse 6 reminds us that God created light when He made the world. Every time He enables someone to "see the light" and become a Christian, it is like a new act of creation. Remember Jesus talking about being "born again"?

Read John 3 v 16–21

Light is a strange thing. Put a bright light outside at night and moths and other bugs will come and gather round it. For other animals, light is danger; they'll stay away from the light and stick to the safety of the shadows. As with light, so it is with Jesus — the light of the world. We're not naturally like moths. We don't like the light. Instead we prefer to walk in the darkness and ignore God. Sometimes we may claim to love God, but are really walking in darkness. Use **1 John 1 v 6** now to check your own "walk" and pray to God about it.

36 – JARS OF CLAY

Paul has spoken to the Corinthian Christians before about God's power being shown in our weakness. Have a look at **1 Corinthians 1 v 18 – 2 v 5**.

▸ *How is the gospel viewed by different people? (v18)*

▸ *Why does the message of the cross seem foolish?*

▸ *But why is it so effective? (v18, 21)*

▸ *What's the great news for those of us who feel useless? (v26–28)*

▸ *What has Jesus done for believers? (v30)*

▸ *So how should that affect their attitude? (v29, 31)*

▸ *How does Paul describe the way he shared the gospel with them? (v1–4)*

▸ *Why did he do this? (v5)*

God hasn't chosen you because you're clever or successful or gorgeous or holy. What a relief! If we trust in Jesus, God accepts us despite all our failings. And He can use us in great ways. But we need to expect a negative response to the gospel much of the time while remembering God's wisdom and power behind it.

37 – WHAT REALLY MATTERS?

▸ *Why does Paul describe his severe sufferings (see chapter 6 v 4–10) as "light and momentary" in v17?*

▸ *What is more important to him? (v17)*

▸ *How does that help you picture how amazing Jesus' perfect kingdom will be?*

38 – PAUL GETS IN TENTS

Paul has written to the Corinthians on this topic before. Remind yourself of **1 Corinthians 15 v 35–57**.

▶ *What will our new bodies be like?*
▶ *Who will we be like?*
▶ *Why do we no longer need to fear death?*

39 – THE GOSPEL TRUTH

Read verses 14–17 again

▶ *How great is Christ's love and how personal is it? (v14)*
▶ *What is true for every Christian? (v17)*

Christians can say as Paul did: "Christ died for everybody, and He died for me". And since Jesus died in our place, there's no way we can go on living self-centred lives, is there (v15)?

Read verses 20–21

Jesus is no longer present on earth in person, so we act as His representatives. We speak on His behalf (v20).

▶ *What was His message? (v20–21)*
▶ *Which words here tell us this job is urgent?*

To be reconciled to God will involve asking Him for the forgiveness He's provided through Jesus. Now, people will make their judgment about Jesus by what they see in His ambassadors (first Paul, then us).

▶ *How are you getting on as an ambassador?*
▶ *Talking about Jesus? Living for Him?*

PSALMS

40 – PRAISE GOD!

Here's a 5 word summary of Psalm 103: *"God rules, cares. Praise. Obey."*

▶ *Can you do better?*
▶ *What difference would it make if God ruled but didn't care for people?*
▶ *Or cared but didn't rule?*

David's completely overwhelmed with God and His goodness. Yet he didn't know of Jesus' coming or that He would die on the cross. See how excited Paul got about that: **2 Corinthians 5 v 14–21**

▶ *What are you thankful to God for?* Tell Him!

41 – CREATION CELBEBRATION

As sinful human beings, we're always tempted to think more of the visible creation than the invisible God. The purpose of Psalm 104 is to glorify God, rather than His creation. Praising the one behind all this amazing stuff!

▶ *In what ways do people idolise creation rather than the Creator?*
▶ *How can we be different?*

Read 1 Kings 4 v 29–33

▶ *What did Solomon's God-given wisdom enable Him to do?*
▶ *Does God think studying biology etc is a waste of time?*

Now read Psalm 104 v 14–15, 23

Knowing who God is actually gives us the best understanding of our place in His world and the best motivation for treating

115

it properly. It's His world! Ask God to give you the right attitude to His world and your place in it.

42 – FAITHFUL FATHER
Read verses 1–5 again

The psalm writer packs so much in these few short verses. It's like a mini guide to godliness: give thanks; call on His name; tell others; sing to Him; rejoice; look to the Lord; seek His face; remember what He's done.

▶ *Which of those do you need to work harder at?*

MATTHEW

43 – KING OF CONTROVERSY
Read verse 16

For Jesus' hearers, many who seemed to be "first" (in with God) were in fact "last". For example, the rich man from the previous chapter and the Jewish leaders who hated Jesus. Shocking! And then, later, even non-Jews (Gentiles) would enter into a relationship with God ahead of people in Israel. God has a wide reach!

▶ *Are you working for Jesus, doing what He wants?*

▶ *Are you a grateful Christian or a grumbling one?*

44 – POWER SERVE
Read verses 25–26 again

▶ *Why do most people want to make it to the top?*

▶ *What reversal of values is Jesus talking about?*

▶ *Will you check your motives for doing stuff?*

▶ *When did you last put aside personal ambition to let someone else come first or get ahead of you?*

▶ *Do you help others just to get noticed and to feel good?*

▶ *How often do you give in when there's a battle of wills?*

Majesty and meekness. Greatness in service. The Creator who's prepared to be murdered by His creation. Remember what that death achieved (v28) and thank God. Ask Him to help you be a true servant.

45 – BLIND FAITH

Already we've seen how God's values are totally different from the world's. Yesterday, we saw the disciples greedily vying for top spot and showing their blindness. Here the blind men show their vision – realising who Jesus is and turning to Him for help. The crowd, who can see, seem to be blind as to who He is. Especially the most "important" ones such as the Pharisees. The first will be last and the last will be first.

46 – ROYAL VISIT
Read Zechariah 9 v 9–17

(Zech' is two books back from Matthew.)

▶ *Why the huge joy? (v9)*

▶ *What would their King be like and what would He do? (v9–10)*

God promised to send a perfect King to rescue His people. But Jesus wouldn't be the usual warrior king. He'd arrive on a donkey, not a warhorse, and His reign would bring peace, righteousness and rescue. He would rule over the whole earth (v10).

God will restore His people and then use them to defeat His enemies. The message of Jesus is peace with God for those who trust in Him, but destruction for those who fight against Him. We need to remember both sides of the gospel. And as you struggle to tell people the truth, you can take comfort from verses 15–17. God will protect you and one day you'll sparkle like a jewel in a crown for Him!

47 – TABLES TURNED

Read Psalm 8

Jesus, God's Son, became the perfect man. He ruled over God's creation and is now crowned with glory and honour. Jesus is our great King. Use Psalm 8 to praise God for how awesome He is, to thank Him for caring for you and for sending His Son Jesus as the perfect King.

Read Hebrews 2 v 5–9

▶ *How does this build on Psalm 8?*
▶ *Why is Jesus now crowned with glory and honour? (v9)*
▶ *Why was Jesus' death so special?*

48 – WITHERING WORDS

Check out Micah 7 v 1–7

The picture is of harvest time. Micah is looking for *"fruit"* — people who still live for God.

▶ *What does he find instead? (v2–3)*

▶ *What will God's visit bring? (v4)*

For these disobedient people, God's visit would bring panic and confusion — complete social breakdown (v5–6). But in the middle of intense misery comes verse 7. Suddenly Micah stops wallowing, and looks on the bright side.

▶ *What hope does Micah cling to?*
▶ *What does he know about God and what He's like? (v7)*

In discouraging circumstances God can still be trusted. He is committed to His people, promises and purposes. Ultimately, we see this in Jesus. Through Jesus, God offers us salvation — rescue from sin. What a bright side!

50 – FRUITLESS CONVERSATION

Read Isaiah 5 v 1–7

▶ *Who is the vineyard owner?*
▶ *What shows how much he cared for it?*
▶ *Yet what happened? (end of v2)*
▶ *What more could God have done for His people?*
▶ *Yet how did they respond? (v4, 7)*
▶ *So what was the verdict? (v5–6)* >>>

God had done everything He could for His people, yet they responded disgustingly. God had done so much for them and so expected justice and right living from them. Instead, He saw violence and distress. But let's not look down on the Israelites for the way they treated God. We need to make sure we don't do the same. God's done even more for us — He sent His Son to die for us and rescue us. And if we respond as the Israelites did, then we deserve destruction too.

51 – WEDDING YELLS

Read verses 8–10 again

This is one of Matthew's big themes: Jesus has come for all. There would no longer be barriers to being one of God's people.

- ▷ *Why must we keep trying to give out God's invitation?*
- ▷ *Why should we pray for people to become disciples, not just converts?*
- ▷ *Do you know what the difference is?*

52 – TAXING QUESTION

Look at verses 19–21 again

The Roman denarius coin had an image of Emperor Tiberius Caesar on one side. On the other side it said: "Tiberius Caesar Augustus, son of the divine Augustus". It was claiming Emperor Caesar was a god and should be worshipped. In distinguishing clearly between Caesar and God, Jesus was cleverly attacking the idolatrous claims made on the coins.

53 – SEVENTH HEAVEN

Read 1 Corinthians 15 v 35–58

God overcomes death every time a seed sprouts to life (v37–38). So raising the dead is easy for God. Everything God has created has been given the right body for its situation (v38–41). And when Christians are raised to live with God for ever, they'll be given new, perfect bodies (v42–44). We've been made in Adam's

likeness but when we're raised to eternal life we'll be made like Jesus ("the last Adam") with new spiritual bodies.

- ▷ *What can Christians expect to happen? (v51–52)*
- ▷ *Why don't we need to fear death?*
- ▷ *If all this is true, how should Christians live? (v58)*

Only God knows when all this will happen. But we have His promise that it will, and that we'll be more like Jesus. Until that day, life can be a hassle, but we know we're on the winning side over death and our own sin (v57). Jesus has already won victory for Christians, so they should live lives that show this — standing firm and giving their all to serve Jesus.

54 – THE GREATEST

Read Deuteronomy 6 v 1–9

- ▷ *Why should the Israelites live God's way? (v1–3)*
- ▷ *How does v4 describe God?*
- ▷ *How should God's people respond to Him? (v5)*
- ▷ *What should they do with God's words? (v6–9)*
- ▷ *Why?*

Wow. Moses hits us with loads of big stuff here. *"The Lord is one"* (v4) — God is the only true God and should be the only one His people worship, love and obey. That's why God's people must treat His words seriously: teaching them to kids and talking about them all the time.

56 – HORRIBLE HISTORY

Write your own (probably much shorter!) version of Psalm 106. Follow these steps.

1. **Rewrite verses 1–5, giving reasons why we should praise God and tell people about Him.**
2. **List some of the times you've let God down badly.**
3. **Remember times He's been far kinder to you than you deserve.**
4. **Say sorry to God and thank Him for His forgiveness through Jesus.**
5. **To finish, rewrite v48 in your own words.**

2 KINGS

57 – DECLINE AND FALL

**Read verse 2 again
then 2 Chronicles 24 v 17–27**

2 Kings only hints at what happened, but 2 Chronicles reveals Joash's chronic change of heart. 2 Kings is raising the question: When's a truly good king coming? When is God's promised King coming? When would there be someone finally to sort God's people out?

▶ *How is this book beginning to point us to Jesus?*

58 – ELISHA BOWS OUT

Read verses 20–21

This dead man was brought back to life after contact with Elisha's bones. God showed that His power, which had been with Elisha, had not disappeared from Israel, even though Elisha was now dead. There is still hope for Israel.

59 – SLIDE RULE

Read 2 Kings 14 v 23–29

Jeroboam II made Israel wealthy and successful. But this had devastating effects on God's people. See what God's prophet Amos said about it...

Read Amos 6 v 1–7

▶ *What was God's criticism of Israel's leaders (v4–6)?*

▶ *What will their punishment be (v7)?*

These guys had an easy life. But they weren't serving God or helping out the poor and needy. They spent all their time stuffing their faces, playing music, getting drunk and beautifying themselves.

Ever fall into that trap? Living only for your own enjoyment and leaving God out of the picture? But God would take it all away from the Israelites and kick them out of their country (v7).

▶ *What selfish things in your life will you drop?*

▶ *Think of things to do instead that please God.*

60 – THE TIDE TURNS

Read what God thought about Ahaz in Isaiah 7 v 1–17

▶ *What was God's message to Ahaz? (v4, v9)*

Aram (AKA Syria) and Israel (AKA Ephraim) got together against superpower Assyria and tried to bully Ahaz into joining them. But God told Ahaz to forget about politics and trust God to rescue His people. Ahaz

119

refused, so God spoke again.

ⓘ *What did God want Ahaz to do? (v11)*
ⓘ *But what did He do? (v12)*

God's angry response (v13–17) sounds weird but it was a picture message. The virgin (God's people) would give birth to a son (a faithful remnant who trusted God) and God would be with them. But Ahaz (and anyone who refused God's help) would face God's punishment. Verse 14 points us forward to Jesus (Immanuel) who'd be born as a human baby — He would be God living with His people. Ahaz refused God's help so Judah would face the consequences. No one and no part of the land would escape God's judgment.

61 – THE END FOR ISRAEL
Read Deuteronomy 28 v 49–68

ⓘ *What was the deal if Israel ignored God's law?*
v49–52:
v58–59:
v62:
v64:

God's people continually rebelled against Him and eventually He kept His word and punished them, as we've seen with the destruction of Israel and scattering of the Israelites. The result of sin and rejecting God's ways was to lose all the blessings He promised His people, and a return to slavery (v68). Rejecting God means being cut off from His perfect plan. This was the stark choice the Israelites had:

- Obeying God would bring a life full of God's blessings.
- Turning from God would bring God's punishment.

62 – HOPE FOR HEZ
Read 2 Kings 18 v 4, then Numbers 21 v 4–9

ⓘ *What is the issue in v4–5?*
ⓘ *Why is v5 such an awful thing to say?*
ⓘ *What is God's response — firstly in judgment and then in mercy? (v6–9)*
ⓘ *What does this tell us about God?*

Those who trusted what God said turned to the rescue He provided (v9). The same offer is open to us through Jesus. Have you accepted it yet?

Now read John 3 v 13–15

ⓘ *What does Jesus say about the bronze serpent?*
ⓘ *What problem did the bronze serpent deal with?*
ⓘ *What problem does the cross deal with?*
ⓘ *What did the Israelites have to do to be saved?*
ⓘ *What about us?*

63 – ROOTS OF RECOVERY
Read verses 21–28
Sennacherib insulted God and boasted of his own achievements, but it was all part of God's plan. God would save His people and restore His honour. The Lord showed the Assyrians exactly who was boss by wiping out thousands of them as well

as King Senna. And the news was good for God's people — God would keep His promises and a remnant would survive. This was King Hez's finest hour — he realised that God was King and nothing was impossible or hopeless. Think what it will take for you to submit to God's rule like this. Will you recognise He's in charge now, or learn the hard way?

64 – GOOD NEWS BAD NEWS

Read what Hez wrote after God cured him from his illness in **Isaiah 38 v 9–22**.

▷ *What do the four images in v12–14 say about how Hez felt?*

▷ *But what brought an amazing turnaround? (v15–16)*

▷ *How did he view his suffering? (v17)*

God rescued Hezekiah from death. Guess what, He does the same for us! On the cross, Jesus defeated sin and death for ever. Everyone who trusts in Him will live for ever with God.

65 – GOOD NEWS BAD NEWS

Read 2 Chronicles 33 v 1–20

▷ *How low did Judah sink during Manasseh's reign? (v9)*

▷ *How did Manasseh treat God? (v10)*

▷ *What changed things? (v11)*

▷ *What effect did all this have on the king? (v13)*

▷ *How did he show he'd changed? (v14–16)*

66 – RAIDERS OF THE LOST BOOK

Zephaniah was God's prophet during Josiah's reign.

Read Zephaniah 1 v 1–6

God would act personally in devastating judgment against the world, and specifically against His people, Judah. But Zeph brought good news too...

Read Zephaniah 3 v 9–20

An amazing turnaround for God's people. God's day will be a day of judgment. And of rescue, too — God will keep a people for Himself, just as He's promised. One day, God's people will enjoy all God's got for them. But how could God just take away their punishment? On the cross, Jesus took God's judgment on Himself, for us. He died to rescue us from what we deserved. That means we can face God's final judgment day securely, knowing that Jesus has rescued us.

67 – READ AND LEARN

For more details of Josiah's life, reforms and death, check out **2 Chronicles 34–35**.

68 – THE END?

If Zedekiah had listened to the prophet Jeremiah, he'd have save both Jerusalem and himself.

Read Jeremiah 38 v 14–28

▷ *What's the choice Zedekiah has to make? (v17–19)*

▷ *What are the consequences?*

▷ *How does v20 summarise the offer God's making Zedekiah?*

▷ *How does v28 show us what Zedekiah chose to do?*

Weak-willed Zedekiah kept consulting Jeremiah in secret, but never acted on what he was told from God. The consequences were devastating. Zedekiah needed to turn back to obeying God (repent), and to trust God would rescue him (believe). Instead he chose to obey his own plan, and trust in himself.

Read Mark 1 v 14–15

Ⅾ *How's Jesus' command here similar to Jeremiah's in 38 v 20?*

Ⅾ *What will this command mean for you and for people you know?*

JUDE

69 – FIGHT FOR THE FAITH

Read the whole of Jude

Ⅾ *What was Jude's original reason for writing? (v3)*

Ⅾ *Why did he change his mind? (v3–4)*

Ⅾ *Why do you think he includes so many reminders in v5–16?*

Ⅾ *What does Jude really want his readers to do? (v3, 20)*

Ⅾ *What will this involve? (v21–23)*

Ⅾ *Why are v1 and v24–25 so encouraging in the light of v3–19?*

70 – GOSPEL GATE-CRASHERS

Read verse 4 again

Making grace an excuse for sinning is covered by Paul in **Romans 6 v 1–14**. Check it out. Jesus died on the cross to take the punishment we deserve. He died for our sin. So when you become a Christian, you have all your wrongs forgiven by Jesus. It is as though your sinful life has died with Jesus. You no longer want to disobey God; you want

to please Him. That's the plan, anyway.

Christians share in Jesus' death and also in His risen life. They are dead to sin — it no longer rules them. It's as if they have become fully alive to God for the first time. Verse 10 calls this living to God instead of living to sin.

Ⅾ *In your attitude, have you drawn a line under sin or have you left the door open to it coming back?*

Ⅾ *Yes, we still fail — but what can you do to kick sin from your life?*

Ⅾ *How can you be more committed to living for God?*

71 – STRONG WORDS

Read verse 9–11

These guys were shooting their mouths off about stuff they didn't understand, including the occult. But even chief angel Michael didn't accuse Satan. That's God's job, not ours.

For the O.T. bits in v11...
Cain — Genesis 4
Balaam — Numbers 22–24; 31 v 6
Korah — Numbers 16
Lots of confusing references and examples in today's section, but the point is simple — taking the wrong way, rushing into error, leads to destruction.

72 – FIGHTING TALK

Read 2 Peter chapter 2

Ⅾ *What connections are there with what you've read in Jude?*

▶ *How does Peter urge Christians to stand firm? (v4–10)*

74 – CRY OF VICTORY

Only with God can Israel gain the victory; without Him they have no chance. But as Christians, we're not facing battles with Edomites or trying to conquer lands for God, so how can this psalm teach us?

Read 1 Corinthians 15 v 24–26 and v55–57

▶ *What enemies do we have?*
▶ *Can we defeat them in our own strength?*
▶ *Who can?*

2 CORINTHIANS

75 – 2 CORINTHIANS CONTINUED

Paul is teaching nothing new here. See what Jesus had to say to His disciples in **Mark 8 v 34–37** and **Mark 10 v 28–31**.

76 – CONTINUATION SITUATION

Unequal marriages were the bane of Israel's life back in the Old Testament. Even kings like Solomon did it (see 1 Kings 11 v 1–9). And despite God warning them again and again, His people kept getting dragged away from Him by hooking up with foreign lovers and adopting their false gods. While no cultures or ethnicities are off limits for Christians today, the New Testament is very clear that believers should only marry other believers (1 Corinthians 7 v 39), for exactly the same reasons.

77 – JOY RIDE

Are there any Christians you feel this way about? Have you ever experienced the joy of introducing two Christian friends and seeing how well they get on? Or maybe you've invited someone to youth group, CU or a Christian camp, and seen how much they've enjoyed it and how they have moved forward in their faith. Pray for deep Christian friendships in your life that will be a mutual encouragement.

78 – GIVE GIVE GIVE
Read Philippians 2 v 5–11

Jesus is worth it — He's God! But He gave up everything He deserved and was humble enough to die on a Roman cross to serve others.

▶ *So what does that mean for us? (v5)*

Here's our motto for life — not "*because I'm worth it*" but "*my attitude should be the same as that of Christ Jesus*". We live Jesus Christ's way by copying His attitude.

79 – GIVE AND LET GIVE

When you first become a Christian, you know you have nothing to offer God and everything is an undeserved gift. But as time goes on, we need to remind ourselves that this is always the case. If we can receive humbly and thankfully from God, it will help us not to be proud and self-sufficient when we need help from our Christian brothers and sisters.

80 – GLEEFUL GIVING

Ever thought about what you will give your money to? What do your parents/church give to? There are loads of charities out there but you need to consider what you think are the most important causes. For example, only Christians give to Christian charities, whereas lots of people care about the environment or re-homing abandoned cats. Also, if we believe that everyone needs to hear about Jesus then maybe supporting organisations who share the gospel would be a good idea...

81 – THINK THANKS

Who can you thank God for, who has given time, money and/or skills to help you, your youth group or your church? Spend some time doing that now.

82 – CHOOSE YOUR WEAPONS

It's so tempting to want to fight back and retaliate when people attack us. How can we show Christ in these sorts of situations?

Check out **1 Peter 2 v 21–24 and 4 v12–19** for some ideas.

83 – FRAUD SQUAD

It's not wrong for Christian ministers and teachers to be supported by their congregations. See **1 Timothy 5 v 17–18** (although notice Paul doesn't take up this right in 1 Corinthians 9 v 9–15). Neither is it acceptable to be stingy in our support of those who care for us spiritually. As one mean church once said of their vicar

— "You keep him humble, Lord, and we'll keep him poor!" But monetary gain should never motivate Christian service (see 1 Timothy 3 v 1–3).

84 – BOASTERS

There are still many, many Christians who are suffering for following Christ round the world today. Get some details from a website like **www.opendoorsuk.org** and ask God that persecuted believers would know God's strength in their weakness and sufferings.

85 – THORNY ISSUES

Read Romans 8 v 28–39

Why not commit some of these verses to memory? They can really help when we encounter hard times.

86 – FOLLOW THE LEADER

▷ *What should our leaders be like?*

Take a look at John 10 v 1–18 and 1 Peter 5 v 1–4

▷ *What about us? (1 Peter 5 v 5–6)*

87 – WORRIED WORDS

We need to keep on repenting and believing in Jesus every day. Take some time out now to confess your sins to God. Remember that Jesus' death paid the price for every sin. Think about how much it cost God to forgive you, and thank Him. Then ask for His help to live for Him — be specific about areas in which you struggle and need His help.

88 – TESTING TMES

People can often worry about whether they are really Christians. On one level, if you are worrying, you probably don't need to! But equally, we shouldn't assume just because our parents are Christians or we go to church that we are OK. Everyone needs to repent of their sin and turn to Jesus for forgiveness individually. Have you done that? Do you now live continually trusting in Jesus for forgiveness day by day? If so, you're a Christian.

89 – SEE YA LATER!

2 Corinthians is a heavy letter — but did it work? Did Paul and the Corinthian Christians get back on good terms? Did they sort out their mess? Well, we have a few clues: we've still got the letter, so presumably the Corinthian guys didn't rip this one up. And when Paul arrived in Corinth, he stayed there 3 months (Acts 20 v 2–3) without mention of any problems (while he was there he probably wrote the letter to the Romans). It's likely Paul and the Corinthians were reconciled. Great!

What have you learnt from 2 Corinthians? Take a bit of time now to skim through the whole letter again, underlining or highlighting any verses or things that have particularly struck you. Ask for God's help to remember them and ask Him to change you so that you are more like Jesus.

90 – ANGRY WORDS

**Read verse 8,
and then Acts 1 v 12–26**

▶ *Who were David's words applied to? (v18–20)*

▶ *What had he done? (v16)*

▶ *Who had he been before that? (v17)*

Now Judas wasn't around — not only had he betrayed Jesus to death, but he himself had died (v18–19). Judas betrayed Jesus. And, like anyone who rejects Jesus, he had to face the consequences.

91 – JUDGE, PRIEST AND KING

Read Hebrews 7 v 17–22

▶ *What does Jesus make possible for us? (v19)*

Jesus' death dealt with sin in a way the Old Testament priests and law couldn't. If we're going to have a real relationship with God, then we need a priest who can make atonement for us to God (pay for our sins so we can be forgiven). And who can represent God to us. That priest is Jesus. He's the better hope.

Jesus has made it possible for us to draw near to God (v19). He's made it possible for us to approach God in prayer; to be forgiven for our sins; to keep going through hard times; to turn to God when we need help; to obey God and live for Him. Jesus has given us access to God — are you making the most of it?

engage wants to hear from YOU!

▶ Share experiences of God at work in your life
▶ Any questions you have about the Bible or the Christian life?
▶ How can we make *engage* better?

Email us — **martin@thegoodbook.co.uk**

Or send us a letter/postcard/cartoon/cheesecake to:
engage, B1, Blenheim House, Longmead Business Park, Epsom, Surrey, KT19 9AP, UK

In the next **engage**

Ezekiel Know God, know hope
James Fantastic faith
Esther God's beauty queen
Matthew End of the road
Plus: The meaning of life
Self-harm / eating disorders
The church – what is it?
Toolbox & Real Lives

Order **engage** now!

Make sure you order the next issue of **engage**. Or even better, grab a one-year subscription to make sure **engage** lands in your hands as soon as it's out.

Call us to order in the UK on 0333 123 0880
International: +44 (0) 20 8942 0880

or visit your friendly neighbourhood website:
UK: www.thegoodbook.co.uk
N America: www.thegoodbook.com
Australia: www.thegoodbook.com.au
New Zealand: www.thegoodbook.co.nz

Growing
with God

Faithful, contemporary Bible reading resources for every age and stage.

NEW!

Beginning with God
For pre-schoolers

Table Talk & XTB
Table Talk for 4-11s and
their parents, *XTB* for 7-11s

Discover
For 11-13s

Engage
For 14-18s

Explore
For adults

All Good Book Company Bible reading resources...

- ❯ have a strong focus on practical application
- ❯ encourage people to read the Bible for themselves
- ❯ explain Bible passages in context
- ❯ cover Bible books in the Old and New Testament

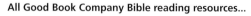
UK: www.thegoodbook.co.uk

N America: www.thegoodbook.com

Australia: www.thegoodbook.com.au

New Zealand: www.thegoodbook.co.nz